# AUSTRALIAN HOMESCHOOLING SERIES

# Basic Economics

## Years 8–10

# CORONEOS PUBLICATIONS

## Item No 564

**This book is available from recognised booksellers or contact:**

**Coroneos Publications**

**Telephone:** (02) 9838 9265    **Facsimile:** (02) 9838 8982
**Business Address:** 2/195 Prospect Highway Seven Hills 2147
**Website:** www.coroneos.com.au
**E-mail:** info@fivesenseseducation.com.au


Item # 564
Basic Economics
by Valerie Marett
First published 2017

ISBN: 978-1-922034-73-1
© Valerie Marett

# Contents

# Section 1

# An Introduction to Personal Finances

# Economics

**Economics is the study of the production and consumption of goods and the transfer of wealth to produce and obtain those goods**. Economics explains how people interact within markets to get what they want or accomplish certain goals.  Since economics is a driving force of human interaction, studying it often reveals why people and governments behave in particular ways.

There are two main types of economics: **macroeconomics** and **microeconomics.** Microeconomics focuses on the actions of individuals and industries, for example, the dynamics between buyers and sellers, borrowers and lenders. Macroeconomics takes a much broader view by analysing the economic activity of an entire country or the international marketplace.

We will start this study with micro-economics and the most basic unit of society, the family.

The aim of this book is to give you an introduction to the world you will live in as an adult, especially in the area of personal finance.

Half of this book will be practical.  You will need to speak with your parents or an other adult and fill in the details as you progress.

# Income

**Income** is the amount of money, or its equivalent, received during a period of time in exchange for labour or services, from the sale of goods or property or as profit from financial investments. The flow of money in the form of cash or cash-equivalents may be received from work (wage or salary), capital (interest or profit), or land (rent).

For most people this will be in the form of wages. However, those, who at the present time do not have a job, have a disability or are elderly may receive money  from the Government. In the case of the elderly this is called a pension. In other cases it may be referred to as a welfare benefit or an allowance.

Speak to your parents or an adult. If they do not want to tell you exactly how much money comes into the family, ask them to set an amount, whose figures you can work within, throughout these exercises.

**Complete:**

| | | |
|---|---|---|
| Wages:   per week: | | _____ |
| per fortnight: | | _____ |
| per month: | | _____ |
| Other monies, e.g., interest, allowance etc. | | _____ |
| **Total income per month** | | _____ |

# Expenses

**We are going to look at expenses individually and you will calculate them as we go along. When we are finished we will chart them all on one page. You will need to look back through the book to do this.**

It is important to understand that **nothing is free**. Everything has a cost. Welfare benefits such as pensions and allowances may be given to individuals or families to help them but they are not free. The tax payer bears the expense. Medicare, hospitals, education etc. are not free. They are paid for by the tax payer.

Everyone who earns income above a set amount, whether through wages, running a business, or investments such as shares or rentals, pays tax. The more you earn, the greater the tax bill up to a point set by the Federal Government.

## Expenses Taken Out Before Wages Are Paid

**Income Tax:** If you are paid a wage your employer will deduct tax each time he pays you. If you run a business the Australian Tax Department will send you a bill every quarter for the amount they estimate you will earn. This is known as PAYG tax, (Pay As You Go). It is usually based on the amount you, as a business owner, earned last year plus an allowance for growth in the business.

To calculate the total amount in tax you would pay on your monthly wage you will need to go to the internet and Google "finding tax payable." Both the Australian Taxation Office and ASIC are safe sites.

Tax per month: _____

**Superannuation:** Superannuation will appear on a pay slip, but is paid by an employer. It is placed into a superannuation account which you can choose, or if you fail to, your employer will choose. Superannuation often does not seem important when you are young but by the time you are 65 years old it will have built up to a sum that will hopefully give you a reasonable income in retirement.

It is important to keep a check on your superannuation. Funds charge fees and some fees are higher than others. These funds are deducted from the superannuation that your employer pays in on your behalf.

If you change jobs you may find that a different superannuation fund has been opened in your name. It is important to roll over your superannuation into one fund. If you do not, the superannuation will eventually be eaten up by fees or the Federal Government will take the money into their coffers.

**Union Fees:** unions are there to maintain and improve the conditions of workers; to protect the disadvantaged; in case of accidents to make sure the person gets their full entitlement in accident pay and to make sure workers are paid their full wages.

The reason we have such good superannuation funds is because unions took interest in superannuation and got on boards to ensure low fees were paid. Unions also became involved in running banks, e.g., Members Equity, to allow members cheaper housing loans and low banking fees.

Unions charge fees but these are proportional to the amount of time worked and are tax deductible.

**Discover what unions charge for membership both for part-time and fulltime members. Find out what benefits they offer.** (The SDA covers hospitality and retail, the industries where many students start their first part-time jobs.)

_____

_____

_____

_____

### VET or HELP repayments

VET or HELP are no interest loans that can be applied for by a student and which is paid by the Government to cover the cost of university or TAFE fees. Regardless of whether a student completes a course, or finds employment in the industry they trained in, once the student starts work and earns above a set wage, repayments will be deducted from their wages by the Tax Department. Repayments vary from 4% to 8% depending on the gross wage. The gross wage is the total amount an employee is paid before deductions are taken out.

**Find out what the repayment thresholds are and what percentage of your wages must be repaid.**

_____

_____

_____

_____

_____

**Complete the following to work out the take home pay per month:**

| | | |
|---|---|---|
| Total wages per month | | _____ |
| Tax | — | _____ |
| Union Fees | — | _____ |
| Any other deductions | — | _____ |
| Total Take Home Pay | = | _____ |

# Basic Living Expenses

## Rent or Mortgage

This is the largest living expense. Everyone has to live somewhere. If you stay at home, parents often charge board to help their children understand that everything has a cost.

**Rent:** A room, a small apartment, unit or a house may be rented. A renter is generally required to provide a security bond and undergo a security check before moving in. They will usually be asked to pay the first month's rent in advance and in some cases may also be asked for the last month's rent.

Both tenants and landlords have responsibilities. The tenant must pay their rent on time; keep the place neat and tidy; respect their neighbour's right to peace and quiet and keep to the terms of the tenancy agreement. (Read this document carefully before signing it.)

The landlord must respect a tenant's right to privacy and comply with entry requirements; carry out any necessary repairs and maintenance and meet all health and safety rules. A landlord can not just evict a tenant. He must give the tenant notice and may have to go to court if the tenant refuses to leave, does not pay his rent or to claim damages.

If you share a house with other people you need to be cautious. You should get to know them well first. The person, or persons, who sign the tenancy agreement are liable for the rent each month. It is not an excuse to say that the person you are sharing with did not pay. **Always get a receipt when paying rent.**

**Find the rent in your area for a decent room, apartment or unit and house per month. If the area you live in is too expensive, find a nearby, cheaper area.**

| | |
|---|---|
| Room | _____ |
| Apartment 1 bedroom | _____ |
| Apartment 2 bedroom | _____ |
| 3 bedroom house | _____ |

**Mortgage:** A mortgage is a loan, usually from the bank, to purchase a house. Most banks require a 5%-10% deposit. The larger the deposit, the better the terms you will obtain, and the lower the mortgage. You will need to show proof of saving over a period of time. You may also be eligible for a Government Grant as a first home buyer.

You will need extra money to cover the initial costs that will include the home loan application fee, possibly mortgage insurance which covers the bank if you default on the loan, Government duties and inspection and conveyancing costs.

How much you can borrow depends on how much deposit you have and your income. Your loan repayments will be based on how much you borrow.

Older houses may prove to be cheaper than new houses, depending on the area. Many older houses will have been done up prior to sale and will include extras like drapes, patios and established gardens.

When purchasing a newly built house it is important to buy from a reputable builder and check what is included in the package. Some packages come with house and land and will usually include a garage but may not include extras like carpets, paths and washing lines. In addition, check how long the build will take.

Before signing any contract, especially one for a house, it is important to read it in its entirety. Do not just accept the word of a sales person that it is a standard contract. If the house is being built you need to regularly check its progress and make sure that each stage meets the contract. If anything has been missed, the builder needs to be notified straight away, as it may be too late to rectify the problem when the building is complete.

The advantage of purchasing a house is that it is an asset you will eventually own. Providing monthly payments are made on time, a home of your own provides housing security.

Whether you rent or purchase a house you will have set up costs for furniture, crockery etc. At a minimum you would need a bed, table and chairs, refrigerator, crockery, saucepans and other kitchen utensils. Some of these may be purchased second hand.

**Find the following:**

| | | |
|---|---|---|
| 1. | The amount a bank will lend based on the total monthly income on page 4 | _____ |
| 2. | The amount of deposit necessary | _____ |
| 3. | The monthly repayment based on the loan | _____ |
| 4. | The cost of: a 3 bedroom house | _____ |
| | a unit | _____ |
| 5. | Initial costs including the home loan application fee, mortgage insurance, government duties and conveyancing costs | _____ |
| 6. | Minimum cost of house set up, e.g., furniture | _____ |
| 7. | Add together the amount in (5) and (6) to calculate the amount needed on top of a deposit | _____ |

# Further costs

**Council rates:** a yearly council rate notice is sent out to home owners. This will include the cost of garbage collections and will be based on the assessed value of your home and land. It can be paid quarterly. This cost will be built into any rental cost. The rates enable the Council to look after parks, maintain roads and footpaths and provide various local facilities.

**Body corporate fees:** this only applies if you have purchased an apartment or unit. The fees will be used to maintain  such things as gardens, parking areas and fences.

**Insurance:** there are 2 types of insurance: **house insurance** on the building and property, which will only be paid by a home owner and will cover fire and accidental or storm damage; and **home contents insurance** which covers those things within the house which are not fixed, e.g., furniture, clothing, jewellery. Even if you rent a house you will want to have home contents insurance.

**Home maintenance and repairs:** all houses need repairs and maintenance at some time.  This includes painting, both inside and out, replacing fences, gutters, tiles etc. If you rent, the owner is responsible for all maintenance. If you own a house you are responsible.

If you purchase an old house, maintenance will generally have to be done either straight away or within the next few years. If you purchase a new house you should not need to do repairs for some time, but there will be many things not covered in the basic home package that you need to pay. Many home packages include basic landscaping in the front and not the back. They do not always include a washing line and never include curtains. They rarely have enough electric sockets or outside hose connections. You will need to factor in these costs.

**Find the following:**

| | | |
|---|---|---|
| 1. | Council rates—divide by 4 to find cost per quarter | _____ |
| 2. | Body Corporate fees on units | _____ |
| 3. | House Insurance | _____ |
| 4. | Contents insurance | _____ |

## Food and General Household Expenses
Food is the second most important living expense since it is indispensable. Include groceries, vegetables, drinks and cleaning products, personal products and other small incidentals in your calculations, e.g., batteries, sticky tape.

**Find the following:**

| | |
|---|---|
| Cost of food and general household expenses per month | _____ |
| _____ | |

## Travel Costs

Unless you work within walking distance of your home you will need some sort of transport. Most young people consider a car to be an essential part of their lives, but if your budget doesn't allow for it, you should consider other means. There are many other means of transport, e.g., bicycle, bus or train. We will compare the costs of these later. If you live in the country transport, other than by car, may not be practical.

**Initial purchase of a car:** the best car to start adult life with is a reliable used car. These are cheaper to purchase and are often more solid than new cars although general maintenance may be higher. When purchasing either it is best to take a parent with you or a knowledgeable, older adult. You will probably be able to save enough money to purchase a used car, which will avoid the need to go into debt. You are unlikely to be able to save the money to purchase a new car and will need to finance it. In that case you will probably need someone to co-sign for you, that is guarantee monthly payments. There will also be an application fee. Many car loans have a fixed interest rate, so the loan is no cheaper if paid earlier.

Cars **depreciate**, that is their value decreases over time. A new car depreciates from the moment you drive it out the car yard, but, at the time you finance the car, with the interest you will pay, the loan is higher than the value of the car. Older cars depreciate at a slower rate.

### Find the following:

| | | |
|---|---|---|
| 1. | Purchase price of reliable, used car | _____ |
| 2. | Purchase price of new car | _____ |
| 3. | Percentage paid if financed | _____ |
| 4. | Cost of car loan per month | _____ |

**Car Insurance:** different insurance policies are needed for used and new cars, but every car owner has a responsibility to insure their car. **At a minimum, a car should have third party property or third party property, fire and theft insurance**. If you have an accident and damage or write off your car, and unfortunately accidents are common occurrences with young, inexperienced drivers, this coverage will ensure you have injured no-one other than yourself. **If you have an accident and damage another person's car, you are liable for that damage.** Having third party property insurance covers you for this type of accident. If you add fire and theft you will be covered if your car is stolen or set on fire.

If you have a new, financed car then you are required to have full comprehensive insurance. This is to ensure that the finance company receives some sort of remuneration if the car is written off as the result of an accident. Comprehensive insurance for a person under 25 years of age or one over 25 years who has not driven a car for four years is very expensive. Even with this coverage there is an excess on the insurance which may be between $1,000 and $1500. An excess is the amount you are required to pay before your insurance company will pay out.

**Maintenance:** cars require regular servicing to run properly. A major service is about $290 and a minor service is about $250. These services will occur every six to twelve months depending on the number of kilometres the car has driven. This does not include the cost of any necessary repairs. Regular maintenance on a car can ensure that it lasts a lot longer.

**Repairs:** as well as parts that wear out, tyres and brakes need to be replaced from time to time. There will also be other repairs that the mechanic discovers when servicing the car.

**Licence and Registration:** generally people obtain a license before purchasing a car. During the time you are a P plater there will be restrictions on your license. At some period your license will need renewing and you will need to budget for this cost.

Car registration is paid each year. If you do not register your car on time you may need to get a roadworthy certificate before you can renew your registration . This is a nuisance you will wish to avoid.

**Road Side Assistance:** while it is not compulsory, joining an automobile club, like the RACV in Victoria, ensures that if you break down you will receive assistance. This is especially useful for women, who may encounter difficulties like changing a flat tyre. Relatives are not always available to help.

**Find the following:**

| | | |
|---|---|---|
| 1 a. | Car insurance 3rd party property (per month) | _____ |
| b. | Full comprehensive insurance   (per month) | _____ |
| 2. | Maintenance costs (per month) | _____ |
| 3. | Estimated cost of repairs | _____ |
| 4. | Licence (per month) | _____ |
| 5. | Registration (per month) | _____ |
| 6. | Total (include only 1a or 1b, not both) | _____ |

**Find the cost of following alternate transport:**

| | | |
|---|---|---|
| 1. | Train (per month) | _____ |
| 2. | Bus (per month) | _____ |
| 3. | Any other possible transport option | _____ |

## Utilities

Utilities include electricity, gas, water and telephone. Whether you rent or buy a house you will have regular bills for most of these. You need to ascertain how often they are sent and budget accordingly. If you rent you may be liable for the water bill as the owner may not have included this in the rent. It is important to check this at the time of renting.

Whether you have a land line or a mobile phone you will have a monthly telephone bill.

### Find the following:

1. Gas bill (average per month)  _____

2. Electricity (average per month)  _____

3. Water (average per month)  _____

4. Telephone/mobile (per month)  _____

## Personal Costs

These include clothes, shoes and hair cuts as well as other personal necessities. Most people own far more clothes and shoes than they really need. Make sure that what you do purchase is good quality and can be mixed and matched with the rest of your wardrobe so that you have a variety of clothes. Make sure you have one really nice outfit with matching shoes for going out somewhere special. Remember you can only wear one set of clothing at a time and money spent on clothing can not be spent on other things like entertainment.

### Find the following:

1. Clothing (per month)  _____

2. Hair  (per month)  _____

3. Other (per month)  _____

## Entertainment

Entertainment includes dinners out or fast food, DVD's, movies, gym clubs, swimming pools entry etc. How much money you spend on entertainment will depend on your budget. If your budget is tight look for cheaper alternatives. Be realistic. Do not spend too much in this area and then not have enough to pay bills.

Entertainment (per month)  _____

# Medical

Whether or not you have private medical coverage you will have medical bills from time to time. These will include chemist, dentist, physiotherapist, chiropractic care etc.

In some states those people who have concession cards are covered for ambulance use. If you do not have a concession card you will need to join an ambulance group like St John's Ambulance. This will cover the cost should you need to use an ambulance and is a small amount per year. If you are not covered you may have to pay thousands of dollars for using this service. None of us plan to be in accidents, but they unfortunately happen and thinking ahead can save huge bills.

**Find the following:**

| | |
|---|---|
| 1. Average medical bills per month | _____ |
| 2. Ambulance cover per month | _____ |
| Total: | _____ |

**Use your totals on the previous pages to add up the basic, unavoidable expenses each month by filling in the following:** (assume you are renting)

| | |
|---|---|
| Rent or Mortgage | _____ |
| Contents Insurance | _____ |
| Travel Costs (car) | _____ |
| Utilities | _____ |
| Personal Costs | _____ |
| Entertainment | _____ |
| Medical | _____ |
| **Total Expenses per month** | _____ |

**To complete your basic budget, fill out the following:**

| | |
|---|---|
| Income per month after deductions | _____ |
| Less Total expenses per month | — _____ |
| Amount remaining | _____ |

Hopefully you had money left in your budget after you have deducted your expenses. This left over money should be saved. If you did not have any money left you need to have a close look at your expenses. **Your parents may pay for many of these expenses at present, but once you leave home you will be responsible for all your own expenses.**

## Savings

You should aim to save between 5% and 10% of your income. Part of this should be allowed to build up into an emergency fund. The unexpected bills can ruin even the most carefully planned budget, e.g., major repairs on a car, replacing the washing machine or refrigerator. The rest of the money should be kept separately. A record of regular savings helps if you later wish to purchase a car or house and apply for a loan.

Be careful where you place your savings. Ordinary bank accounts return virtually no interest. Both Members Equity and AMP provide high interest savings accounts. These are online accounts and provide reasonable interest providing no money is withdrawn during the month. The online savings account is linked to an ordinary savings account and money can be drawn down as needed.

**Fixed Term Deposits**: A term deposit is a cash investment held at a financial institution such as a bank, building society or credit union, for an agreed rate of interest over a fixed amount of time, known as a term. When the money is deposited, the customer understands that the money is there for the pre-determined period which usually ranges from 1 month to 5 years and the interest rate is guaranteed not to change for that nominated period of time. Typically, the money can only be withdrawn at the end of the period. If it is withdrawn earlier a penalty is attached, which may include losing all the interest gained on the money. Banks have recently altered their policy to no longer permit withdrawals unless a case of hardship can be shown.

A fixed term deposit rolls over at the end of the specified period unless the customer contacts the institution and gives them different directions. When a fixed term deposit rolls over, the interest on the new fixed term amount is usually lower than previously.

The Federal Government guarantees up to $300,000 dollars held in any bank. They do not guarantee credit unions or other institutions. It is therefore safer to leave your money in a bank.

**Check the current rate on the following:**

| | | |
|---|---|---|
| 1. | Ordinary savings account | _____ |
| 2. | Online savings accounts | _____ |
| 3. | Best time and rate for fixed term deposit of up to 1 year | _____ |

# Credit Unions

A credit union is a non-profit financial institution that is owned and operated entirely by its members. Credit unions provide financial services for their members, including savings and lending.

Anyone can join and become a member. When a person deposits money in a credit union, he/she becomes a member of the union because the deposit is considered partial ownership in the credit union. Each member of a credit union, mutual building society and mutual bank owns the organisation they belong to, and have a vote in the organisation's governance.

Unlike publicly-listed banks, credit unions aren't publicly-listed companies on the stock exchange and so they do not maximise profits to pay external shareholders. Instead, they put their profits back into customer service, better products, competitive mortgage rates and fairer, competitive pricing for their members.

The money in credit unions is not guaranteed by the Government and over the last 30-40 years a few have become bankrupt. This meant that many of their customers lost large amounts of money.

Find and list 3 well known credit unions. State the interest offered to their customers on ordinary savings accounts and the best rate they offer in fixed term deposits.

_____          _____

_____          _____

_____          _____

# Shares

A share is unit of ownership in a corporation or financial asset. While owning shares in a business does not mean that the shareholder has direct control over the business's day-to-day operations, being a shareholder does entitle the possessor to an equal distribution in any profits, if any are declared in the form of **dividends**.

Shares are generally sold on the **stock exchange.** The stock exchange is a market in which shares of publicly held companies are issued and traded. The stock market is one of the most vital components of a free-market economy, as it provides companies with access to capital in exchange for giving investors a slice of ownership in the company. The stock market makes it possible to grow small initial sums of money into large ones, and to become wealthy without taking the risk of starting a business or making the sacrifices that often accompany a high-paying career.

In the past, shareholders received a physical paper stock certificate that indicated that they owned "x" shares in a company. Today, brokerages have electronic records that show ownership details. Owning a "paperless" share makes conducting trades a simpler and more streamlined process than it was when stock certificates needed to be taken to a brokerage.

**Shares are long term investments. They are not a means of earning quick money.** There are many seminars and books now on "How to Make Money on the Stock Exchange." If the people running the seminars or selling the books were making the money they claim, they would not need to run seminars or rely on book sales as a means of income.

**Share prices fluctuate** with the economy and with customer confidence, however over a long period their value remains or increases. Investment in shares should be approached cautiously. The shares with the best returns are usually expensive but they are solid. Shares that sell cheaply are a much higher risk.

Consult a newspaper or watch the "ordinaries" (part of the news) and find out what are the top 3 shares listed. Write them below along with their sale price.

| | |
|---|---|
| _____ | _____ |
| _____ | _____ |
| _____ | _____ |

# Debt

It is very easy to get into debt and very hard to get out of. The most common forms of debt are credit cards.

### Credit Cards

Credit cards allow you to purchase now and pay later. In return for this service the bank charges a high interest rate. This may vary from 10% to as high as 22% a year. This means that, at the lowest rate of 10% if you spent $500 and only paid the minimum rate by the end of the year you would owe $600 if you did not use the credit card any more. The charges on credit cards are compound interest, that is the amount of the principle will increase each month unless fully paid off.

The rule is **do not spend on a credit card what you can not pay back within the month.** Many debit cards now serve as credit cards when used online. Be careful, some of these allow you to spend more than is in your bank account.

You will see advertised credit cards that offer 0% interest for 12 months. To take advantage of these cards you must now have a minimum balance of $10,000 owing on another card. To get any advantage from this type of card the holder must pay it off in 12 months. The banks are betting that not only will the person not pay off the balance but they will spend more. Any purchase made on the card accrues interest from day one and these must be paid for before any of the transferred money can be taken off the $10,000.

All credit cards charge a flat fee each year for the use of the card. The low fee credit card charges less in fees, but does not allow you to collect reward points like Fly-By points. Fly-Bys are accrued when you shop at particular locations. It takes thousands and thousands of points to get even the smallest reward.

To prevent paying interest on a credit card, the balance must be paid off at the end of the month. To help you understand how much interest it is possible to pay on even a small amount look at the table below. The amount owing on the credit card is $966.89. Assume you will make no additional charges to the card.

| Payment per month | Pay off time | Interest Paid |
|---|---|---|
| Pay full amount | end of month | $0 |
| Minimum payment $25 | 4 years 4 months | $321.65 |
| $46.28 | 2 years | $144.10 |

**Buy Now, Pay Later**
You will often see advertisements that say either "buy now, pay later," "no payment for 3 months" or "buy now and have 2 years interest free." These are designed to get you to purchase a product you can not really afford.

In the case of furniture or white goods like a refrigerator, taking advantage of the offer might be a good option. To gain full advantage from this type of offer you need to work out how much you need to pay each month to clear the debt within the period where no interest is charged.

Look at the following chart. A coffee machine valued at $2,200 was purchased on a 2 year free interest plan.

| Payment | Time Taken to Pay | Interest Charged |
|---|---|---|
| minimum payment | 10 years 7 months | $1935.66 |
| Pay monthly amount | 2 years | $0.00 |

**N.B.** This assumes the monthly payments are paid on time each month. Paying extra each month would clear the debt quicker.

The common practice is for financial institutions to issue a credit card to make repayments easier for the customer. The card has all the features of a credit card and once some of the debt has been paid it can be used as such. **Never** do this or you will find yourself deeper and deeper in debt.

**Payday Loans**

**Never, ever,** be tempted by one of these. A payday loan is money advanced before your next pay day at high interest. Two of the most well known lenders are Nimble and Cash Converters. These lenders promise to come to the customers rescue with a "smart little loan." All of these type of lenders have the same charges as they are governed by the maximum that the Government allows. 20% of the principal plus 4% of the principal per month. If you borrow $100 then you will immediately owe $120. If you do not pay within a month, or the time allotted, you will owe $124.80. By the end of six months, with compound interest, you will owe $149.57—almost half again of the money you borrowed. If you miss a payment there is a penalty. There is a $35.00 fee and if the missed payment is not paid quickly, you will be billed an extra $7 per day. (The amount is capped at 200% of the principal.)

If you are unable to pay a bill speak to the business concerned. You can usually get an extension or work out a repayment plan without exorbitant charges. Alternatively speak to your parents and enlist their help. **Do not borrow cash on these terms.**

**Find the following information:**

1. The current interest paid by you on a
   standard credit card                                        _____

2. Minimum payment each month spending $1,000                 _____

3. Find a furniture or similar company offering a
   12 month or more interest free loan                         _____

4. Choose an item.          Price:                             _____

5. Cost of monthly payment per month over 12 months
   to completely pay for item                                  _____

4. Check out some of the payday loans. Discover
   interest paid each month.                                   _____

5. In a recent advertisement for an instant loan
   a lady claims she had to get this type of loan as
   she needed a new washing machine. List  her other
   alternatives.

   _____

   _____

# Hints on Managing Your Money

1. **Automatic Debits or Set and Forget**: Income is deposited electronically, rent or mortgage payments are debited. You can set direct debits and can pay for almost everything by card. This "set and forget" mentality can allow money to slip through your fingers. Many people allow money to drift in and out of an account without checking. This can mean you are paying for things you are not using, e.g., a gym membership, magazine subscription you no longer receive. Keep direct debits to a minimum and check your bank account each week to ensure you know what you are spending and how much is in your bank. With internet banking this is easily accomplished.

2. **Cash vs Cards:** If you are watching what you are spending, paying by cash may be the best way to keep track. When you use cards to pay it is easy to spend without thinking. If you have cash in your wallet you notice each time you spend because you can physically see the money disappearing. On the other hand using a card does ensure a record of each purchase. If you prefer to do this, use EFTPOS as the card does not allow you to spend money you do not have. Check weekly to see what money is in the account. Keep in mind when you do this that you may have direct debits coming out and there needs to be enough money left to cover these. If these is not enough money you will be charged a hefty default fee.

3. **Fraud:** Check your statements regularly and if there are any transactions you do not recognise contact your bank. Skimming, where small amounts  are fraudulently debited from your card from time to time, can occur and will only be picked up if you check your account frequently. Paywave has made it easier for people to steal from you.

4. **Fees:** Your statement summaries will show the total incoming and outgoings and fees charged. If you are spending more than you are earning you need to cut costs. There are fees for using the ATM's, fees for foreign transactions, account keeping, dishonour fees and more. If the account fees are high, check with your bank to see if there is an account that will cost you less but still meet your needs.

5. **Paper or Digital Statements:** Most companies are asking customers to accept statements digitally and are charging fees for paper statements. Print out, check and file any statements you receive. Statements online are pdf versions of the paper versions and are legally identical. All institutions are required to keep records of statements on file for seven years.

6. **Technology:** Often a good phone plan is cheaper than pre-paid. Consider whether you really need a cellular option on your tablet computer. It can cost $200 connection fee up front and $25 or more per month. We live in a world where wi-fi is almost everywhere and you can use your phone as a personal wi-fi hotspot.

7. **Be Careful What You Commit to:** once you are 18 years old or over you are

legally bound to any contract you sign—a credit card, a lease, or purchasing a car.

8. **Have an Emergency Fund:** This should contain at least $2000. Have a separate bank account for it and build it up gradually until you have $2,000 in it. Keep this purely for emergencies, e.g., major repairs on a car. Do not use the fund when you have overspent. Live frugally until the next pay day.

9. **Little costs add up:** if you cook your meals and take a packed lunch you will save a great deal of money over a year. You will also appreciate the meal more on those occasions when you eat out.

10. **Tricks for being able to purchase a home:** Before you start saving for a home, pay off your debts, e.g., credit cards or personal loan for a car, and do not incur any more. Then put the savings into a separate account you do not touch. Most banks have quite good interest rates and low or no fees on accounts designed for this purpose providing you deposit a set amount per month.

   **a. Have a savings plan:** work out how much you can realistically afford to pay spend on a house, that is how much you can repay on the mortgage each month. Realistically you probably will not be able to afford to live in the same suburb as your parents. Add 2% to the current interest rate to account for future rate rises. Be realistic about your living expenses.

   **b. Set a goal for a deposit:** the larger the deposit you have the better. If you can save 20% of the purchase price you can avoid lenders' mortgage insurance and save a lot on interest repayments.

   **c. Stick to a budget:** be disciplined in this. It may mean going without purchasing coffees and lunches, cutting back on your entertainment costs etc.

   **d. Save before you spend:** If possible have the portion you wish to save direct debited from your salary and paid directly into a savings account. If an employer does not wish to do this you can set up, via internet banking, for an amount to be deducted from your normal account into your savings account.

   **e. Don't expect to get there in a hurry:** Saving the money to purchase a house takes time and discipline but is well worth the effort. Remember, in the end you will either be paying for the mortgage on your own home or by renting, paying for someone else's mortgage. Consider a cheap, small house to start with. You can always sell and buy a bigger house in the future. Older houses in a growing area are often cheaper than new houses and have extras the new houses don't, e.g., patios, curtains.

11. **Credit Cards:** you are better off using a debit card that acts as a credit card rather than having a credit card. When you use a debit/credit card it takes the money straight from your account. Just be careful as even a debit/credit card can be overdrawn. If you choose a credit card, pay it off each month. **The average credit card debt is $4,400. If the minimum amount is paid and the debt is not added to it will take 31 years to pay it off and cost $14,900 in interest.**

12. **Neither a lender or a borrower be:** Apart from major items like a house or car do not borrow money. Under no circumstances lend your friends money or co-sign on a loan for them. **By co-signing on a loan you are committing yourself to pay should the other person default.**

13. **Money is finite:** The only thing that can be guaranteed is the money you have worked for in the previous pay period. No-one can guarantee you will still have a job in the next few months or year because of the present economic climate. With this in mind do not spend more than you earn.

14. **There are no free lunches:** Money may have seemed to appear magically for your parents when you were young but it didn't. All they have, they worked for. If you aspire to a similar or better standard of living you must be prepared to work for it too.

15. **Be Content:** Do not covet what your friends have. Your friends may have the latest in technology, eat out a lot and go to fantastic parties, but you do not know what their financial situation is. The odds are that they are drowning in debt. If you listen to them you will probably find they are not satisfied but are looking for something "new" all the time.

**Look back through the book this far. List <u>at least 3</u> important things you have learnt.**

# Section 2

# An Introduction
# to
# Basic Economics

# Types of Economy

We will now consider the economy itself in more depth. First we need to study the various methods of organising the economy that have evolved over time, as well as methods of increasing production and thereby increasing the standard of living of the community.

The type of economy used within countries is largely a question of the countries' belief about the extent to which the central government should participate in the economic system.

1. **Traditional or Unplanned Economy**

   In this type of system many individuals produce and market goods and services which they consider profitable. They own the land, buildings etc. and hire the labour they need. This is not a Free Enterprise system because a person's freedom depends upon their position in the system. An example of this would be a subsistence level economy, which is a non-monetary economy that relies on natural resources through hunting, gathering and limited agriculture. Trade is only used for basic goods and there is no industrialisation.

   A traditional economy is characterised by many individual plans and no one master plan: there would be no central committee to co-ordinate all projects. This system is governed by the price system: as the system expands, its price is governed by the rise and fall of its markets.

   Traditional societies produce products and services that are a direct result of their beliefs, customs, religions, traditions etc. These areas tend to be rural second or third world countries and are closely tied to the land.

   **Advantages and Disadvantages**: There is minimal waste within this society, but a surplus is a rare thing. The society preserves its traditions and customs. Each member of these societies has a more specific and pronounced role, and the society is often closely knit and socially satisfied.

   This society fits in well with a society advocating maximum personal liberty, that is the idea that we should be free to use most of our income on whatever we desire. It provides an incentive to stimulate new ideas to produce better and more goods.

   The disadvantage is that traditional economies do not enjoy the things other economies take for granted, e.g., Western medicine, centralized utilities, e.g., electricity, trains etc.

2. **Command Economy**

   In a command economy a large part or all of the economic system is controlled by a centralised power. One example of this is communism. In a command system the market plays little to no role in production decisions.

Command economies tend to develop where a country finds itself in possession of a very large amount of valuable resources. The government then steps in and regulates the resource. Often the government owns everything involved in the industrial process from the equipment to the facilities.

**Advantages and disadvantages**: If the government uses intelligent regulations, a command economy is capable of creating a healthy supply of its own resources, which then rewards the people of the country with affordable prices. (Do not forget that these prices are set by the government.) There is generally no shortage of jobs, as government jobs keep on growing as the population grows.

The government in a command economy only wants to control its most valuable resources. Other things, like agriculture, are left to be regulated and run by the people.

3.  **Market Economic System**
    A market economy is very similar to a free economy. The government does not control vital resources, valuable goods or any other major segment of the economy. Organisations run by the people determine how the economy is run, how supply is generated, what demands are necessary etc.

    **Market Economy and Politics:** The biggest advantage to a market economy, outside of economic benefits, is the separation of the market and the government. This prevents governments from becoming too powerful, too controlling and similar to the oppressive governments of the world that oppress their people while living lavishly on controlled resources. One must be wary of a system which must foster constant growth, but as a result progress and innovation has occurred at incredible rates and affects the way the world's economy functions. In the 1960's Australia was a Commonwealth country trading largely with other countries within the British Commonwealth. Today we trade with many other countries, e.g., China and Japan.

4.  **Mixed Economy**
    **Capitalism and Socialism:** *Capitalism* is an economic system based on private ownership of the means of production and their operation for profit. Characteristics of *capitalism* are ownership of private property, capital accumulation, labour for a wage, voluntary exchange, a price system, and competitive markets. No truly free market exists in the world. While Australia is a capitalist nation, our government still regulates fair trade, government programmes, moral business, monopolies etc. The advantage to capitalism is that you can have an expanding economy that is relatively safe and well controlled.

    In contrast *socialism* is an economy in which the government, like a command economy, controls and owns the most profitable and vital industries, but allows the rest of the market to operate freely. Prices are allowed to fluctuate freely based on supply and demand.

In a **Mixed Economy** the government controls certain industries and undertakes certain activities on the grounds of social justice, e.g., the government provides the framework of law and security necessary so that, so called, free enterprise can in fact be free. However government control in a mixed economy goes much further than this because:

a.    certain industries and services are essential, but would not be profitable to undertake, e.g., pensions.

b.    For the security of the country as a whole it is felt desirable that the Government maintain certain industries and services, e.g., water, electricity.

c.    The government undertakes certain activities because in the past public opinion has felt there was a need, e.g., Fair Work Commission.

d.    As a result of the necessity of large scale control during war time and the scale of some of these controls, many of the controls are maintained during peace time as they are felt to still have value.

**Answer these questions;**

1.    List the different types of economies and in one or two sentences define the type of economy.

_____

_____

_____

_____

_____

_____

_____

_____

_____

_____

_____

_____

_____

_____

2. Which type of economy is Australia? Explain your answer.

_____

_____

_____

# Features of a Modern Economy

## A. Divisions of Labour

In a modern economic system workers tend to spend most of their working hours engaging in one particular occupation. As a result some of their needs are satisfied directly by their own efforts. Essentially the meaning of a division of labour is "You do this for me and I'll do this for you."

Today the process of specialisation and the range of goods and services exchanged have increased tremendously from the time when the only means of exchange was barter. (In the first settlement in Australia the means of exchange was rum.) It is the replacement of barter by some form of money, whether it be cash, cheques or paperless exchanges via the internet, which makes possible the expansion of the specialisation process.

In our society each member of the community is dependant upon the rest of the community for both necessities and luxuries. For example, in the case of a desk, the wood for the desk has to be grown at a plantation. The tree was chopped down and transported to the factory where it is sawn up and turned into a desk. In another example, steel is smelted from iron ore and ferrous scrap, then elements such as manganese, nickel, chromium and vanadium are added to produce different grades of steel. These ores had to be mined and the finished steel needs to be transferred to factories for production in  construction, domestic utensils etc.

## B. Industrial Division of Labour

Production in our economy is divided into three main types:
- a.  primary: farming, forestry, fishing, mining
- b.  secondary: processing
- c.  tertiary: services, building industry, shops, entertainment

- The higher the standard of living, the larger are the tertiary and secondary industries because of the demand for luxury products.

- The tertiary industry is at least half of the nation's income.

- The three divisions, primary, secondary and tertiary are all dependent on one another.

## C. Urban and Rural Distribution of Population

As a country makes economic progress and its standard of living increases the proportion of the country's population in provincial and metropolitan areas increases and the proportion in rural areas decreases.
For example:
**1921-1954:** the proportion of people in  rural areas fell from 37% to 21% and those in the metropolitan area rose from 48% to 53%.
**1966:** roughly 18% lived in rural areas as compared to 65% in metropolitan areas.
**2006:** 88% lived in metropolitan areas as compared to 10% in regional areas.

## D. Reasons for Movement of the Population

1. There has been a tremendous development of secondary industry in metropolitan and larger country cities with the resultant increase in employment opportunities in these areas.
2. There has been an increase in mechanised farming and a movement towards larger farms and as a result there are fewer employment opportunities in the country.
3. As cities grow there are greater opportunities for communication and transport industries. These industries attract and increase the population.

## E. Occupational Divisions of Labour

Occupation is the nature of the work the individual performs in person. The nature of specialised industries has seen the development of specialised occupations. In a car factory, e.g., each individual has a specific job and does not assemble the whole car. Generally this has meant that an individual's employment is long term. In other factories an individual may only be packing boxes or processing orders to be sent out on trucks. This requires less specialised skills and therefore jobs may not be as secure.

## F. Advantages of the Division of Labour

1. The greater skill of the workforce can lead to increased output, which results if a workman's effort is directed to the production of only one good or only one phase of production.
2. Natural skills may be used to the best advantage in a large firm where each person is given the job he does best. The result is increased output of a better quality and at a lower cost.

## Disadvantages:

1. It is harder to replace a specialised worker if he is away for a few days sick.
2. The same pride is not taken in work when compared to old craftsmen.
3. Workers may become bored with repeating the same process many times.
4. There is increased nervous strain, especially if the pace is set by a machine.
5. Inventiveness by an individual is checked. If the task is very simple there is no opportunity for the development of inventive genius.
6. The difficulty of organising the work so that all the workers at different stages are kept constantly employed.

## Elasticity of Demand

The term elasticity of demand refers to the change in the amount demanded in response to the change of the price of the good. If in response to a small price change we have a relatively large change in the amount demanded, the demand for that good is elastic. On the other hand if there is little or no change when the price increases or decreases we say the price of the good is inelastic.

The aim in introducing specialisation is to decrease costs, increase efficiency and thereby enabling a price cut in the hope there will be a big rise in demand for a good. If there was a large increase in demand in response to a small decrease in price, the price is **elastic** and it would be worthwhile introducing specialisation. However if the demand for that good was **inelastic**, that is, in response for a small decrease in price there is little or no increase in demand, it would not be worth

Introducing specialisation as it is likely that the large increase in output could not be sold.

## Technical Progress

With the introduction of electricity, industries were no longer confined to areas around the coal field. (Coal was bulky and expensive to transport.) Electricity could be transmitted all over the country and as a result factors like closeness to markets and labour supply could be considered when deciding the location of an industry. Industrialisation was sped up by the introduction of the assembly line. The technique was adopted in industries where the product was standardised and where demand can be expected to increase greatly if the price is lowered.

### Answer these questions:

1. What is meant by a division of labour?

_____

_____

2. What division of labour occurs within your own home?

_____

_____

3. Complete: In our society each member is _____ on the rest of the community for both _____ and _____.

4. List the three main types of production in our society and explain what they are.

_____

_____

5. Explain briefly in your own words the reasons for the movement of the population from rural to more urban areas.

_____

_____

_____

6. Define "occupation."

_____

7. Define "elasticity" in terms of economics.

_____

8. What is the aim of specialisation?

_____

_____

9. What was the main change that allowed factors like closeness to market and the labour force when locating an industry?

_____

## Organisation of Industry

In a modern economy the size of both individual firms and the industries themselves are increasing. Large scale units of production has been brought about largely by the creation of joint stock companies. Joint stock companies make it possible for the use of thousands and thousands of dollars of capital to be obtained from the shareholders willing to contribute in joint ventures. This is in contrast to the early manufacturing enterprises where one person provided most of the capital.

This however creates the problem of separating ownership from control of the capital since obviously thousands of shareholders can not control the day to day activities of the firm. This is overcome generally by having a board of directors accountable to shareholders.

Another problem that occurs in large scale enterprises is the difficulties confronting management, e.g., difficulties of co-ordinating all activities of the firm. Such activities often result in waste and loss to the firm. However the size of the firm need not be a disadvantage if the quality of management and managerial techniques grow as the firm grows.

It is often claimed that more efficient production within a firm is a result of economies of a large scale. While this is so in many firms it may be due more to the increasing size of the industry. Large industries provide work for certain external economies, that is:
a. banking, finance, transport
b. skilled labour force
c. subsidiary firms, e.g., producing parts for industry or ship yards
d. research organisations and trade missions.
e. the government is more likely to help a large and wanted industry, e.g., ship building industry than help a small, unwanted industry, e.g., pizza shop.

Another form of organisation in industry is the establishment of industrial combinations. In Australia there has been a considerable development in the growth of combinations and monopolies due to various factors including:
a. Horizontal combinations, that is the amalgamations of firms once in direct competition. A current example is Coles who owns Bunnings and Kmart. Directors on boards of different companies are often interlocking, e.g., newspapers run under various names but the two main newspaper owners are News Corps Australia and Fairfax.

b.    Vertical integration, i.e., bringing various stages of production under one control.

c.    Lateral integration, i.e., marketing a product in a different way. Over the last fifty years advertising has changed from being in newspapers, radio and television, to television and on the internet.

d.    Oversees markets. Australia exports to many overseas markets around the world and an increasing amount of food in supermarkets is sourced from overseas   even if it is grown here.

a.    Combinations of firms within Australia may be international in character, e.g., Holden, Toyota. A cartel is a combination of firms trading under their own name but accepting price regulation, production quotas and marketing zones as laid down by the central controlling agency of the cartel, e.g., Holden is controlled from the USA and Toyota from Japan. These cartels may be a danger if their policies conflict  with government policies in the international relation sphere.

Other features of a modern economy include:
a.    the growing strength of organised labour
b.    the increasing intervention of governments in the economic sphere.

## A.  Complete the following:

1.    Large scale businesses have been brought about by the creation of

_____ companies.

2.    Prior to this _____ provided the capital for manufacturing enterprises.

3.    Large industries provide work for external economies such as : _____,

_____, _____, _____, _____,

_____  _____.

## B.  Answer these questions:

1.    Shares are sold in large companies to raise income. What problems occur as a result of both selling the shares and having a larger company?

_____

_____

2.  What types of combinations of businesses and factors are found in Australia.? Explain briefly what each is.

_____

_____

_____

_____

_____

_____

_____

_____

_____

_____

## Production

Production is an activity directed to the satisfaction of people's wants through exchange, usually of money.

This definition has been reached over the centuries by three main stages:

a. In fifteen century England a common view was that only primary producers should be called producers. It was claimed that others only increased their wealth by changing the form of things produced by primary industries, e.g., a flour mill only changed the wheat already produced.

b. Adam Smith, in his "Wealth of Nations" extended the meaning of production to include all secondary as well as primary industries because, in his opinion, production should include all forms of work which contributed to the making of some form of material product. He excluded all people whose work had no connection to material goods, e.g., plumber.

c. Today we do not consider goods to have been produced until they are in the hands of the consumer. All who contribute to any stage between the production of the raw material and the final product are said to have provided productive services, e.g., merchants, retailers, transport, delivery services, manager etc. Furthermore doctors, lawyers etc. who do not produce goods, but who provide material services for which people pay are considered service providers. However unpaid service, e.g., housewives, produce grown in vegetable gardens etc. would not be included in estimating production in the technical sense.

### The Productive Process

This is the name given to the way in which the economy is organised so that the producers are able to supply the goods and services that their community wants. It is the way in which the economic process is carried out, i.e., the production and purchase of goods and service, is shown in the diagram at the top of the next page.

Production is undertaken to satisfy demand:

a. The volume of services and goods produced is governed by the amount of spending.

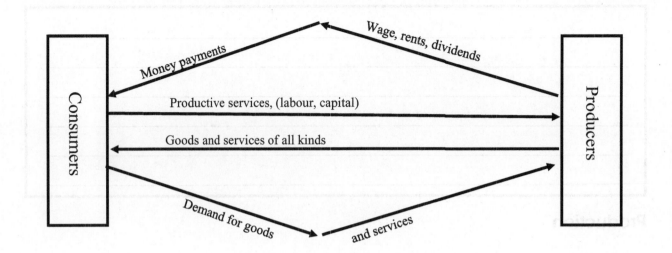

b. The amount spent by persons, governments and businesses depends on their income and on the expectations concerning the size of their income in the future, e.g., how much a person spends in purchasing a house. The size of their income at present depends on the payments they receive for their product or services. The payment may be wages, salaries, rents etc. —the person who repairs the machinery in a factory would receive a wage and the manager of the factory would receive a salary.

c. In return for their contribution to national outcome, people receive payments which enable them to buy goods and services and this represents their share in the distribution of national income. A producer, e.g., a farmer, represents national output.

**Note:** all people are consumers and some may also be producers. Those who consume but don't produce fall into the following categories:

- dependents of consumers, e.g., spouse and children.

- pensioners, retirees.
  In either case there is a redistribution of producers income to support these people who can not support themselves.

- goods and services demanded are of two types:

  (i) consumer goods, e.g., food and clothing

  (ii) producer goods, e.g., raw materials, factory machinery.

**Answer these questions:**

1. Define production.

_____

_____

2.  What is the productive process?

_____

_____

3.  What affects how much producers decide on how much to produce?

_____

_____

4.  Explain the difference between a wage and a salary.

_____

_____

_____

5.  Make a list of a range of products people consume.

_____

_____

6.  Make a list of a range of products people produce.

_____

_____

7.  What does the amount spent by persons, governments and business depend on?

_____

_____

8.  What happens if the amount spent by persons, governments and business is in excess of what they earn?

_____

9.  Since 2008, Australia has developed a deficit, that is the Government spends more than it earns. Based on your answers in question 7 and 8, is this sustainable? What does Australia need to do if it is to be prosperous?

_____

_____

10. Google: Australian deficit 2016. A graph will show you that we went from a surplus in 2008 to a deficit from 2009 until 2016. 50% of the population receives some sort of payment or salary (Government bureaucrats), from the Government. How many percent are supporting these payments? Is that fair?

_____

# Historical Forms of Economic Organisation

The various economic organisations that existed in the past provided the foundation of modern economic organisations. The following information is to help you see how our modern system gradually evolved.

## Feudal System

Serfs were allotted a piece of land by their lord and in return, as payment, went to work on the lord's property a set number of days each week. They were also expected to give him a percentage of their produce. Villages were self-supporting and families had to satisfy their own wants directly.

The Black Death caused the deaths of half the population of England and therefore created a shortage of labour. This gave the labourers the leverage to bargain with the lords to pay rent in money instead of goods. This meant many lords found it more profitable to grow wool rather than wheat. As a result the land was fenced in for sheep, the labourers lost their common land where they could graze and no improvements were made in agriculture.

## Guild Systems

Although secondary industries and trade developed in the late middle ages, agriculture was still the main activity of many people in towns and the difference between the towns and villages was mainly a matter of size.

As manufacturing developed in various forms, citizens of a town would ask permission of some authority, usually the King, to establish a merchant guild, whose function was to control trade in the interest of the town. This control was on the basis of a local monopoly. These guilds were self-governing and a very close association, maintained control over quality and price and they bound members to the guild's regulations.

The guild decided whether strangers could buy and sell in the town. They also decided the conditions surrounding the transactions and made treaties with other towns, either in England or on the Continent.

A specialised type of guild, the craft guild, appeared about the thirteenth century and gradually replaced the merchant guild. The new guilds contained craftsmen of one trade only.

### Organisation of the Craft Guild

1. The membership was compulsory for the masters, journeymen and apprentices.
2. The assembly, council and warden controlled the guild's offices.
3. Members of the guild could be fined, suspended or expelled.
4. The apprenticeship was usually for seven years. They lived with the master and had instruction in citizenship as well as craftsmenship. They received little pay.

**Functions of the Craft Guild**
1. To control every phase in their particular industry.
2. They did a great deal of social and charitable work among their members.
3. They helped ease unemployment and quietened arguments preventing legal action.

The masters worked alongside the journeymen and apprentices, but in later years the masters became merchants and ceased working as craftsmen.

Journeymen were prevented from leaving their masters and so in self-defence they formed Journeymen's Guilds.

Note the similarity between the masters working beside their employees, while organising the production and sale of the goods and the employers in modern industries, e.g., a master builder often works alongside his employees while still organising his business.

# The Domestic System
This was the chief type of industrial organisation after the guild system and before the factory system.

### Features of the Domestic System of Industrial Organisation
1. Clean division between capital and labour.
2. People were paid on a piecemeal basis.
3. A big advance in specialisation.
4. Territorial division of labour, that is, special types of products were made in different areas.
5. The beginning of the factory system by assembling workers under one roof.

# The Factory System
This was one result of the era known as the Industrial Revolution. Although there were great changes in the method of production in the second half of the eighteenth century, it wasn't until the nineteenth century that the factory system finally evolved, therefore the revolution was a gradual change, not a sudden one.

The reasons behind the great industrial change during the late eighteenth century were:
1. Stable government and sufficient freedom of enterprise, both of which were necessary to make industrial progress possible.

2. Capital was necessary in large amounts for industrial expansion and wealth was available at this time due to availability of natural resources and accumulation due to wealth from past successful business.

3. An adequate labour supply was a necessity and this was available as a result of improvements in agriculture led to a decline of labour needed on farms.

4. The start of a rapid growth in population.

5. Improved means of transport and better banking facilities.

The development of more efficient methods of production, due to mechanical inventions, was thus made possible by the factors listed above. This led eventually to a change in the structure of industry.

1. As part of the Industrial Revolution the factory system gradually replaced the domestic system, that is, handcraft production under the domestic system was replaced by machine production. However this change was a gradual one and was slower in some industries than others, e.g., the mechanisation of the wool industry was not completed by the mid nineteenth century.

2. Another feature of the new factory system was that workers were employed as permanent wage earners, instead of being paid piecemeal. The employee no longer owned the equipment they worked with as they had under the domestic system, nor did they work at any other job as they had previously.

3. Power was applied to the machines under the factory system: first water power and then steam. This had an effect on the location of industry since it was necessary to locate factories near the source of power. The industrial north and the midlands became the centre of English industry.

4. The introduction of machine production led to the specialisation and expansion of new industries.

5. One of the not so good features of the factory system meant that employees often lived and worked under very bad conditions. However by the end of the nineteenth century there had been great improvements in this area.

6. Trade unionism first achieved importance during the period in which the factory system was established, although the growth of the movement was hampered by laws against trade unions.

7. The factory system and the more efficient production methods associated with its development enabled Britain to undertake an enormous increase in output. The increase was so rapid that she could support her population and increase its standard of living despite the fact her population increased fourfold between the eiteenth and nineteenth century. Furthermore her exports of industrial goods had increased to such an extent that by the early nineteenth century these goods were being purchased throughout the world and it wasn't until the end of the nineteenth century that her technical knowledge and industrial achievements were being seriously challenged by other European countries and North America.

Answer these questions:

1. Read through pages 34-35. Under the headings of Feudal System, Guild System, Domestic System and Factory System list the main features of each.

a. Feudal System: _____

_____

_____

_____

_____

_____

b. Guild System: _____

_____

_____

_____

_____

_____

_____

_____

_____

c. Domestic System: _____

_____

_____

_____

_____

_____

d. Factory System: _____

_____

_____

_____

_____

_____

_____

_____

2. Of the systems mentioned, which type of system best describes the system in modern Australia?

_____

_____

© Valerie Marett
Coroneos Publications

Australian Homeschooling #564
Basic Economics

# Distribution of National Income

## Primary Production

Look at the following terms and their meanings:

1. **Australian primary production** includes wheat, cattle, dairy products, other agricultural products, fisheries, forestry and minerals.

    a. The **gross value** of primary production is the value of the production at the market.

    b. The **local value** of primary production is gross value less marketing costs.

    c. The **net value** is the local value less materials.

2. **Marketing Costs**
    a. Freight
    b. Packaging
    c. Commissions

3. **Raw Materials**
For example: fodder, sprays, dips, petrol, oil.

4. **Distribution of net value**
Costs such as wages, insurance, rent, rates, tax have to be taken out of the net value and items such as interest paid on loans need to be added.

Looking at the terms used above you can see that while a farmer may have lots of sheep or cattle, for example, which on paper, may appear to be quite valuable, they do not have any real value until they are sold. When the farmer sells them he has to deduct the cost of getting them to market from the price he is paid, (local value.) The money left is still not profit because to find the actual profit (net value) of the sheep or cattle the farmer needs to deduct the cost of raising them. These costs include hay or grain feed, de-worming, vaccinations. For example using simple figures:

|  |  | $ |
|---|---|---|
| Sheep Sold | = | 15.00 |
| freight |  | - 3.50 |
| raising sheep |  | - 9.00 |
|  |  |  |
| profit |  | 2.50 |

**N.B.** These are not accurate prices. They are used to show how little profit a farmer makes per sheep.

## Secondary Industries

These include such things as sugar, rice, fruit and vegetables, and manufacturing of all kinds. Look at the following terms:

## Distribution of value in secondary industries

1. **Value of output of a secondary industry** is the wholesale selling value at the factory of goods made or processed during the year including by-products. It also includes other work done, e.g., repair work to a factory or upgrading of equipment, which makes the industry more valuable. For example, we did little upgrading over the years of our oil refineries. This has led to the shutting down of many of the processing plants and phasing out of others as we are unable to compete with the new refineries in Singapore.

2. **Value of production** is the value of the output, (what is produced,) less the value of raw materials and the fuel used. Raw materials include containers, tools replaced, stores used etc. Fuels used include coal, gas and electricity.

### Distribution of the value of Production
Any money received would be distributed firstly to meet other expenses involved and secondly to pay for labour and loans used in the cost of production.

Other expenses would include an allowance for depreciation, payroll tax, superannuation, rent and advertising. The proportion of the value of production devoted to these expenses and the proportion going to labour and capital depends on the industry concerned. In an industry where advanced mechanisation has occurred, the capital would probably absorb a much greater proportion than labour.

The proportion of the value of production being distributed to capital may be done in the following way:

1. As interest payments on loans made to the business.

2. As profits paid to the owners of the capital, e.g., shareholders.

3. By increasing capital equipment, that is, ploughing back the profit into the firm.

## Tertiary Industries
Tertiary industries are mainly service industries and include:

1. professional services

2. education (This is one of our largest tertiary industries.)

3. public administration

4. domestic services

5. transport

6. merchants and retailers

7. builders and construction

The value of tertiary industries are distributed similarly to secondary industries. For example in a shop 50% would go to pay for suppliers and service providers, e.g. electricity; 25% would go to labour; 15% to capital, leaving little profit.

In the case of an electrician there would be more profit as the cost of supplies might only be 15% and the capital 25%. He might work by himself or emply one other person so the labour cost might be as low as 15%, leaving him a much larger profit.

In the case of professional services the value of production is mainly in the form of wages or salaries.

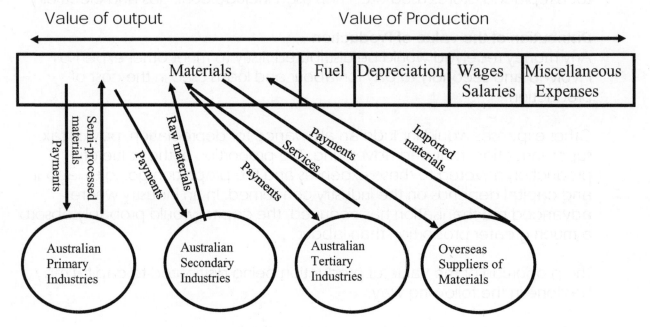

A. Draw a line from the terms in the first column to the correct definition in the second column. The terms all refer to primary production.

|  |  |
|---|---|
| 1. gross value | a. local value less materials |
| 2. local value | b. wages, insurance etc. taken out of net value |
| 3. net value | c. freight, packaging commissions |
| 4. marketing costs | d. value at the market |
| 5. raw materials | e. gross value less marketing costs |
| 6. distribution of net value | f. fodder, sprays, dips, petrol, oil |

B. Answer these questions:

1. Give 3 examples of the following:

   a. Tertiary Industry: _____

b. Primary Producer:_____

c. Secondary Industries: _____

2. Think carefully. Where you live depends on what industries can be found near you and governs the jobs available, e.g., if you live in the country you are more likely to be near primary producers; if you live in the city you are more likely to be near secondary and tertiary industries. List as many primary, secondary and tertiary industries that can be found near your home. (within 40 km.)

_____

_____

_____

_____

_____

_____

_____

_____

_____

_____

_____

_____

_____

© Valerie Marett
Coroneos Publications

Australian Homeschooling #564
Basic Economics

# Trade Unions

Trade unions may be defined as a **continuous** association of **wage earners** for the purpose of maintaining and improving the **conditions** of the worker's lives. Trade unions not only began in the nineteenth century but also undertook the first Australia-wide conflict between organised capital and organised labour, This was the start of the tradition of labour solidarity.

The various trade union origins and organisations have been many and varied, and as a result, much of the trade union history after this early development has been devoted to consolidating and bringing the different trade unions together as an organised section of the workforce.

## Periods in Trade Union History

### 1. Pre 1850
Before 1850 Trade Unions were of little significance in Australia because there were no secondary industries; people were spread out and there were a large amount of workers who were convicts.

### 2. 1850-1860
The real start of the Trade Unions dates from the gold rush period of the 1850's. Although Trade Unions were in existence before this period they were of little significance.

### Reasons for the lift in status of the Trade Unions

1. During the 1850's there was mass migration of people to the gold fields who brought with them the traditions of the English union organisation from countries where they were already established. These men provided the knowledge for founding our Trade Unions.

2. Trade Unions were in a strong position at this time because demand for labour always exceeded the labour force.  More and more labour was needed to provide for the needs of a rapidly expanding population and to replace pastoral workers who had left for the gold fields.

A weakness of the Trade Unions during this period was that many of the unions grew up in isolation. There were many factors involved, but the main one was that they were patterned on English craft unions. Union leaders often thought of immediate objectives which may have conflicted with long term objectives. Further more these objectives were not always in the best interests of the labour movement as a whole. Unions at the time were more interested in work conditions than in increasing wages, which were already high due to the abundance of gold.

### 3. 1860-1890 strikes
Features of this period were:
a.  Gold production was declining and there was much unemployment, both

in the primary and secondary industries.

b. Unions struggled to maintain wages and increase better working conditions. It was the unions during this time that helped obtain restriction acts against the Chinese. It was felt that the Chinese undercut the wages of Australians and that they did not help the Australian economy as most of their money was sent back to relatives in China.

c. Between 1870-1890 Australia experienced a period of rapid economic development, and unions, along with other sections of the community, prospered. Unions were strongest in the cities.

d. Unions began to combine more on a national basis. For example, in 1869 the first conference of union delegates representing the six Australian colonies were held in Sydney.

e. Unions obtained legal status between the period 1876—1902.

## 4. Period of the 1890 strikes

Prices dropped after a boom period and employers cut wages. Non-union labour was readily available. During the period 1890-91 both the Maritime Union and the Shearers Union went on strike. The employers were supported by the State, the press and the Church. As a result employers exploited the situation and tried to make the unions ineffective. In retaliation the Shearers Union and Maritime Union combined to boycott non-union wool.

The strikes were defeated with the return of the Maritime Union to work, but these strikes laid the framework for the Australian Labor movement's entry into parliamentary politics. The New South Wales Labor Defence Committee summed up the union's mood in this statement: "the time has come when trade unionists must use the parliamentary machine that in the past has used them".

## Labour in Politics

In the early stages labour members were few and the unions merely supported the party that was most sympathetic to labour views. But by 1890's the policy of the party was more clearly defined and members were more united in their support.

The Queensland branch of the Australian Labor Federation had already begun organising to endorse parliamentary candidates in 1890, and the first local branch was formed in Fortitude Valley in February 1891.

Meanwhile, in 1890 the NSW Trades and Labor Council, through its parliamentary committee, was already drafting a constitution and rules for a new party to contest elections in 1891. The first local branch is claimed for Balmain, in April 1891. In both colonies the new party was the creation of the trade union movement, especially of shearers, but with many other unions participating.

In 1892 the NSW Labour Bureau was established and was the first NSW

Government agency to deal with employment-related issues. It predominantly focused on providing job opportunities and accommodation for the unemployed. In 1895 the Bureau was absorbed into the NSW Department of Public Instruction.

The Factories and Shops Act 1896 was the first comprehensive regulation of working conditions in factories, shops and other industrial establishments. The legislation restricted the working hours of women and children. Later in 1899 the Early Closing Act 1899 restricted the length of working hours for all employees. Monday to Thursday shops could remain opened until 6pm; Fridays they might stay open until 10pm and Saturdays they must close by 1pm. Shops were closed on Sundays.

## 5. Twentieth Century Developments

Three Acts of significance appeared in 1901. The "Industrial Arbitration Act 1901", when the first 'modern' industrial relations statute came into force. A separate Arbitration Court was established, with binding arbitration powers.

The Apprentices Act, 1901 created the basis for the administration of all apprenticeships in NSW and reduced the hours of apprentices to a maximum of 48 per week and the Shearers' Accommodation Act, 1901 set standards for the accommodation of shearers and others engaged in pastoral occupations.

In 1907 the basic wage was set for male employees only. The Federal Harvester Case established a basic wage for male workers on the basis of their 'breadwinner' status. In the 1912 Fruitpickers Case the Federal Commission rejected an argument that male and female basic wage be equal. These decisions were followed by all Australian industrial relations tribunals.

By 1908 the "Industrial Disputes Act 1908" replaced the 1901 Industrial Arbitration Act and introduced "Wages Boards" that could determine pay and conditions applying across all industries.

Later the Commonwealth Government was enpowered under the Constitution to set up a Tribunal for the prevention and settlement of industrial disputes extending beyond the limits of any one state. The idea was to replace force as a weapon in settling disputes between labour and capital. The Act provided for registration of Interstate or Federal Unions. In the **Reconciliation** process both the union and the employer were brought together by a third party. If no agreement was reached in the **Arbitration Court** both cases were heard by a judge who rendered a binding decision.

**Answer these questions in your own words:**

1. Why were trade unions unimportant before 1850?

_____

_____

2. What changed in the 1850's? How did the country change?

_____

_____

_____

_____

_____

3. Why did Trade Unions start to develop during the 1850's?

_____

_____

4. Why did Trade Unions prosper between 1870-1890? Give 2 reasons.

_____

_____

5. Complete: Union obtained legal status between _____.

6. What laid the frameworks for the Australian Labor Party's formation? Explain your answer.

_____

_____

_____

_____

7. The Factories and Shop Act was passed in 1896. Why was it important? What were its provisions?

_____

_____

_____

8. In 1899 the Early Closing Act restricted the length of working hours for all employees. Research what is now considered the maximum ordinary working hours for the week and what hours these apply to.

_____

_____

## The Australian Council of Trade Unions

This was established in 1927 as a permanent federal authority, although delegates from various states had already been meeting before the strikes of the 1890's. A constitution was adopted creating the A.C.T.U. It stated that this was to be the supreme governing body of the trade union movement, and its decisions were to be binding on all affiliated bodies.

Trade and union councils had already been established by 1927. Most local unions are connected to trade and labour councils, to which they send delegates when meetings are held. When the A.C.T.U. was established these trade and labour councils became branches.

A Congress is held biannually. Decisions made at these Congresses include:
    a.    the level of wages
    b.    working conditions
    c.    trade union policy on national and international matters.

Trade and union councils administer A.C.T.U. policy within their own states. Furthermore they are the final authority in handling matters that are only of concern to their state.

The Executive of the A.C.T.U. is made up of 60 members, although in the beginning there were only 16 members.

## Objectives of the A.C.T.U.
The objectives are:
    a.    the socialisation of industry.
    b.    the organisation of wage and salary earners in the Australian work force within the trade union movement.
    c.    the utilization of Australian resources to  maintain full employment, establish equitable living standards that increase with output, and create opportunities for the development of talent.

The A.C.T.U. adopt various methods in carrying out these objectives. They  have established the idea of one union for one industry, that is closer organisation of workers by converting from the old craft basis to the industrial basis. The craft unions consisted of people of one trade, e.g., bricklayers, while the industrial union consisted of the people of one industry, e.g., Australian Builders Labourers Federation. This policy can be seen through the tendency of the number of unions to decrease while for many years the number of unionists have increased. In the last twenty years membership in unions have declined to a record low.

The A.C.T.U. has introduced the idea of unified controls, administration and action as a means of consolidating the Trade Union movement. They also advocate centralised control of industrial disputes.

A **World Foundation of Trade Unions** was established in Paris in 1945. The democratic countries broke away from it on the grounds it was communistically controlled and they formed the **International Confederation of Free Trade Unions**.

## The Achievements of the Australian Labour Movement
Three main things have been achieved by the Labour Movement.
    a.    increased wages

b. decreased hours
c. better working conditions

Four main methods have been employed by the labour movement to achieve these aims:
    a.    strikes
    b.    arbitration
    c.    collective bargaining
    d.    political power

The A.C.T.U. has played a large part in labour achievements in that it has converted the Trade Unions into a powerful bargaining force. Employer associations, e.g., Chamber of Commerce and Industry or Chamber of Manufacturers, have also developed considerably over the same period. However the employers' influence on history has not been as strong as the trade union movement. This is because employers have always joined together as a defensive measure in an attempt to control labour activities. There has been very little  positive development by employer movements.

Employers' positive aims have included:
    a.    advancement of the trade interests of employers, e.g., acting as pressure groups to obtain political concessions to assist employers generally or employers in a particular industry.
    b.    improving public relations to advance the interests of their association.
    c.    formation of monopoly devices, e.g., restrictive trade practises to protect their members.

## Some problems  with Trade Unions

1. **Wage Problems:** the basic aim of the trade union movement is higher real wages for their workers. An increase in a workers' wage would be of little use to workers if price levels in the economy were rising rapidly. In such circumstances it is likely that the workers' real wage has actually fallen. This is because the price rises may be so great that, even allowing for the wage increase, the worker can no longer purchase as many things as before. It is the duty of the union to see that the workers receive the highest wages that can be justified by the prosperity of the industry.

It can be dangerous to increase wage levels when the economy can not afford it because:
    a.    the increase in costs to the firm can in time force the less efficient firms out of business resulting in the loss of employment of their workers.
    b.    alternatively the employers may decide to meet the extra cost of wages by raising the price of their product. If the goods are necessities all workers suffer an increase in the cost of living.
    c.    Firms may attempt to decrease costs by substituting, where possible, machines for men. As a result workers are dismissed.
    d.    The firm may decide to manufacture their product overseas where labour

costs are cheaper. Again, as a result workers are dismissed.

e.  Higher production costs may mean that Australia increases its export prices and is now a weaker competitor for overseas trade.
f.  Those on fixed incomes always suffer the most because real wages and incomes are falling.

These problems may be avoided if:
a.  firms produce more efficiently and avoid raising their prices.
b.  if workers increase their output to counteract rising costs.

2.  **Hours of Labour:** the aim is to increase leisure while not decreasing production. In actual fact production is likely to increase if the hours worked per day are decreased or limited. This is because if a worker works long hours his efficiency falls and therefore production falls. Under such circumstances if hours are decreased then productivity may rise. However this argument is not valid in Australia today as the working hours are not excessive and labour efficiency is near maximum.

The 40 hour week was introduced in 1948 following a decision by the Commonwealth Arbitration Court. Other tribunals have extended it to cover most industries not covered by this award.

On July 24th, 2014 the working week was further reduced to 38 hours.

3.  Incentive Schemes: incentive schemes are set up by some employers to keep valued employees with the firm, e.g., paid maternity leave, additional superannuation.

Since the 1990's there have been a decreasing number of people joining unions. This can be seen in the decreasing number of working days lost to strikes. Some of this is due to the fact that many migrants are happy with the conditions in Australia. It is also partly due to the fact that whether or not a person belongs to a union, the gains made by unions will automatically be passed on to all workers in the industry.

**Research further and then write an essay outlining both the advantages and disadvantages of unions. Include references to different times in history and compare with other countries, e.g., USA, where there is limited or little union power.**

_____

_____

_____

_____

_____

_____

_____

_____

_____

_____

_____

_____

_____

_____

_____

_____

_____

_____

_____

_____

_____

_____

_____

_____

_____

_____

## The Industrial Relations Commission

In 1904 the Conciliation and Arbitration Act was set up. Its function was to hear and arbitrate industrial disputes and make awards. It also could interpret and enforce awards and hear civil or criminal cases relating to industrial law.

Its early role was to resolve disputes that extended beyond state boundaries. In practise this became a "paper war" where unions would write to employers with a log of claims or a log of demands. The Employer would then reject all or part of the demands, creating an industrial dispute. This dispute would then be arbitrated and the result of arbitration was an industrial award.

During the first twenty years of their role it became clear that this court should exercise broad jurisdiction over a range of industries. In 1926 the Act was reformed and among other provisions, it stated that all cases involving the basic or living wage would be heard by a full bench of the Court. The change also allowed for the appointment of Conciliation Commissioners, whose role was similar to mediators.

The Court was abolished in 1956 following a decision of the High Court in the Boilermakers' case. The High Court held that the Conciliations Court could not exercise both an arbitration and judiciary role.

Following the decision two new bodies were created to take over the functions of the previous court: the Commonwealth Conciliation and Arbitration Commission, which in 2006 became the Australian Conciliation and Arbitration Commission, was to carry out non-judicial (mediation) functions; and the Commonwealth Industrial Court, which later became part of the Federal Industrial Court, and was created to carry out judicial powers.

Throughout its time the Commission created Awards which covered a whole range of industries. This acted as a system of minimum wage setting in Australia. The Commission also registered a large number of trade unions to assist in the Award formation processes. The Commission is famous for its cases of equal work and equal pay as well as decisions on unfair dismissal and redundancy pay.

Throughout the period from 1904-2006 the Australian Industrial Commission created Awards which set the minimum terms and conditions of employment for people who worked for certain employers. A standard award would have approximately 20-30 conditions and was about 40 pages long. The Awards would be reviewed periodically.

The Australian Industrial Relations Commission would also certify enterprise bargaining agreements. These agreements were negotiated contracts usually between a union, as representatives of employees on the site, and an employer of the site.

In addition they would register trade unions and deal with demarcation disputes. They would also deal with unfair dismissal applications.

Under the Rudd Labor Government, the Australian Industrial Relations Commission was abolished. Its functions were transferred to a division within Fair Work Australia in January 2010.

## The Commonwealth Basic Wage

In 1907 the minimum wage to be paid to unskilled workers was 42/-. This amount was agreed when a bill was drawn up to force employers to pay a fair and reasonable wage to their employees.

In 1953 the quarterly wage adjustments were abolished and replaced with a yearly adjustment of the minimum wage. Automatic price adjustment was abandoned as it was thought that it aided inflation because as soon as the public was given more money (in the form of wages) prices rose.

Inflation has two main causes:

a.    demand for goods, which causes price rises.
b.    cost inflation: workers obtain higher incomes and this causes the cost of products and services to rise, lowering the value of money.

The Australian Industrial Relations Commission and now the Fair Work Commission are in an important position in wage setting. This has a huge influence as more than half of the wage and salary cases in Australia are under Federal Awards. Historically the state bodies have looked to them for leadership, and are reluctant to move too far out of line with them. Decisions on the level of wages are made according to the capacity of industry to pay. They look at productivity as a means of determining capacity to pay.

## Margins

The **basic wage** is defined as the lowest wage that may be paid to any worker of any industry under the Commonwealth Awards. An amount paid above this is called a **margin** and is paid for skills and/or responsibilities. The amount depends on the capacity of the industry to pay; the amount of skill and responsibility and a comparison with rates overseas and in other industries. Adjustments become necessary when the value of money becomes less. In 1959, for example, the workers of the metal trades were granted a 28% margins increase. This was granted because the workers were considered to have increased productivity in the industry and they deserved something in return.

## Wage Price Index

A Wage Price Index (WPI) survey is used to construct the WPI, a measure of changes, over time, in retail prices of a constant basket of goods and services representative of consumption expenditure by resident households in Australian metropolitan areas. These changes are not affected by the quality and quantity of work. It was found necessary in 1960 to change the basket. This new index was called the **Consumer Price Index** (CPI) which allowed for 263 items to be included, 150 more than before.

It is used by a wide range of organisations and individuals in industrial relations forums, developing wage policies and economic analysis. WPI is the major measure of inflationary pressures on wages and salaries and is one of the preferred information sources when assessing monetary policy.

The steps for finding the WPI are:
- a. make a base period
- b. make a "basket of goods"
- c. give more weight to some items if necessary
- d. calculate the total cost as a percentage.

The following example shows how the WPI is used to calculate rises in wages.

|  | Index No. |
|---|---|
| June quarter 2012 | 112.5 |
| Less June quarter 2011 | − 108.5 |
| Change in index points | 4.0 |
| Percentage change | 4.0 ÷ 108.5 x100 = 3.7% |

The rise in wages between the June quarter 2011 and the June quarter 2012 was 3.7%.

## Changes in the Living Conditions of the Australian Worker

Examining this involves the examination of the following economic factors:
- a. level of wages
- b. working conditions
- c. social services

### Level of Wages

The real level of wages is the purchasing power of money and goods for services. Since there have been almost continual increases in the general level of prices during the second half of the twentieth century and up until the present day, it is often argued that while there has been large increases in wages over this period, the value of real wages had altered little.

### Working Conditions

Amenities in factories have improved including first aid provisions, rest periods, penalty rate, paternity leave and paid maternity leave. Although working conditions are better, taxation is heavier.

### Social Services

People are now assured of a safety net if they are unemployed or disabled. Single parent benefits and old age benefits are also available.

### Answer these questions:

1. What was the purpose of the Conciliation and Arbitration Act?

_____

_____

2. Explain the reforms made to the Act in 1926.

_____

_____

3. When was the Court abolished? Why? What took its place?

_____

_____

_____

_____

4. What is the High Court? (If you don't know, find out.)

_____

_____

5. Complete: In _____ the Australian Industrial Relations Commission was abolished and replaced with _____.

6. Quarterly wage adjustments were abolished in 1953 with a yearly adjustment of the minimum wage. What was the reasoning behind this change?

_____

_____

7. Explain the term "margin" when it refers to wages.

_____

8. What does the CPI measure? Explain fully.

_____

_____

_____

9. Think! Research. Discuss with adults. Then answer the following question. Explain some of the changes in Living Conditions of the Australian worker since the end of World War 2 in 1945.

_____

_____

_____

_____

_____

_____

_____

_____

_____

_____

_____

_____

_____

_____

_____

# The Australian Banking System

The financial systems of Australia can be divided into the following:

a.  **Reserve Bank of Australia:** it conducts monetary policy, works to maintain a strong financial system and issues the nations bank notes. It commenced operations as Australia's central bank on 14th January 1960.

    It contributes to the stability of the currency, full employment, and the economic prosperity and welfare of the Australian people. It does this by setting the cash rate to meet an agreed medium-term inflation target, working to maintain a strong financial system and efficient payments system, and issuing the nation's banknotes.

    The Reserve Bank provides certain banking services as required to the Australian Government and its agencies, and to a number of overseas central banks and official institutions. Additionally, it manages Australia's gold and foreign exchange reserves.

b.  **Banks:** Provide a wide range of financial services to all sectors of the economy, including (through subsidiaries) funds management and insurance services. Foreign banks authorised to operate as branches in Australia are required to confine their deposit-taking activities to wholesale markets. Their money is partially guaranteed, up to $300,000 by the Australian Government. The largest banks are NAB, Commonwealth Bank, ANZ and Westpac.

c.  **Building Societies:** building societies raise funds primarily by accepting deposits from households. They provide loans, mainly mortgage finance for owner-occupier houses and payment services. Traditionally they have been mutually owned , they are increasingly issuing share capital.

d.  **Credit Unions:** are mutually owned institutions. Credit unions provide deposit, personal/housing loan and payment services to members.

Australia's banking system has few banks but many branches. This system of banking is known as branch banking. Unit banking, where there are small, independent banks that have few, if any, branches, are found in the Midwest and Southwest USA.

**Answer these questions:**

1.  What type of banking system do we have in Australia? Explain what the name means.

    _____

    _____

2. List the jobs of the Reserve Bank. (Research if necessary.)

_____

_____

_____

_____

_____

3. What are the major differences between banks, building societies and credit unions?

_____

_____

_____

_____

_____

_____

_____

_____

_____

_____

_____

_____

4. Discover and write below the names of banks, building societies and credit unions in your area. If you are in a country or remote area chose a reasonable sized town to base your answers on.

Banks: _____

Building Societies: _____

Credit Unions: _____

# History of Australian Banking Before the 20th Century

1. In 1817 Governor Macquarie granted a charter to the first Australian bank: the Bank of New South Wales, (now Westpac.)

2. By 1841 eighteen banks had been established due to the prosperity of the rapidly expanding wool industry. The number of banks was excessive and droughts, decreasing wool prices and a serious fall in land values resulted in

several banks becoming bankrupt and closing.

3. The 1851 gold rush brought a great increase in wealth and population. As a result eight new banks were founded.

4. 1863-1878 twelve new banks came into existence due mainly to the prosperity of existing banks rather than to the expansion of the Australian economy during this time.

5. The land boom of the 1880's resulted in the formation of a further thirteen new banks. Australian banks were operating in a free-banking system, and, in addition to few legal restrictions on the operation of banks, there was no central bank and no government-provided deposit guarantees.

6. The commercial banks lent heavily, but following the asset price collapse of 1888, companies that had borrowed money started to declare bankruptcy. The depth of the banking crisis became apparent when the Federal Bank failed on 30 January 1893. By 17 May, 11 commercial banks in Sydney, Melbourne and other locations across the country had suspended trading.

7. Until 1910 banks could issue private bank notes, except in Queensland which issued treasury notes (1866–1869) and banknotes (1893–1910) which were only legal tender in Queensland. Private bank notes were not legal tender except for a brief period in 1893 in New South Wales. Queensland Treasury notes were legal tender in that State. Notes of both categories continued in circulation until 1910, when the *Australian Notes Act 1910* prohibited the circulation of State notes as money and the Bank Notes Tax Act 1910 imposed a tax of 10% per annum on 'all bank notes issued or re-issued by any bank in the Commonwealth and not redeemed'. These Acts put an end to the issue of notes by the trading banks and the Queensland Treasury. The *Reserve Bank Act 1959* expressly prohibits persons from issuing bills or notes payable to bearer on demand and intended for circulation.

8. In 1910, the Australian pound was issued—approximately $2— and was the legal tender in Australia.

9. The Commonwealth Bank was established in 1911 by the Federal Government and by 1913 had branches in all six states. In 1912, it took over the State Savings Bank in Tasmania and did the same in 1920 with the State Savings Bank in Queensland.

10. The Great Depression of the 1930s brought a string of bank failures. In 1931, the Commonwealth Bank took over two faltering state savings banks: the Government Savings Bank of New South Wales (est. 1871) and the State Savings Bank of Western Australia (est. 1863). In 1991, it also took over the failing State Bank of Victoria (est. 1842).

11. From the end of the Great Depression banking in Australia became tightly regulated. Until the 1980s, it was virtually impossible for a foreign bank to establish branches in Australia; consequently, Australia had very few banks.

**Answer these questions:**

1. What was the first bank opened in Australia? Is the bank still open?

   _____

   _____

2. The development of what Australian industry led to the establishment of further banks?

   _____

3. Why did so many banks come into existence and then later collapse during the period between 1841 and 1893? Think carefully. Not all reasons are mentioned in the text.

   _____

   _____

   _____

   _____

   _____

   _____

   _____

   _____

4. What problems were encountered with bank notes before 1910?

   _____

   _____

5. The history of banking in Australia up until World War II was a series of "up's and down's" with no central regulation of banking of any kind until 1910. Would you agree or disagree? Give your reasons.

   _____

   _____

   _____

   _____

   _____

# Development of Central Banking in Australia

The Commonwealth Bank was established in 1911 to carry on the general business of banking in competition with the existing trading banks. It was to be a savings and trading bank. A Governor was placed in charge of the bank and was not to be subject to political control, except in minor matters. At that time, the note issue was administered by the Australian Department of the Treasury, which had taken it over from the private trading banks and the Queensland Government.

In 1924, the *Commonwealth Bank Act* was amended and the Bank was given control over the note issue. Management was then vested in a board of eight directors, including *ex officio* the Governor and the Secretary to the Treasury. From this time until 1945 (when there were major changes to the legislation), the Bank gradually evolved its central banking activities, initially in response to the pressures of the Depression in the early 1930's, and later by formal, although temporary, expansion of its powers under wartime regulations. These included exchange control and a wide range of controls over the banking system (including authority to determine advance policy and interest rates, and to require private banks to lodge funds with it in special accounts).

The new *Commonwealth Bank Act* and the *Banking Act*, both of 1945, formalised the Bank's powers in relation to the administration of monetary and banking policy, and exchange control. Under the 1945 legislation, there ceased to be a board, which was replaced by an advisory council of six, comprising entirely officials from the Bank and the Treasury; the legislation specified that the Governor was responsible for managing the Bank.

However, legislation in 1951 established a new board (at that time of ten members), including the Governor, Deputy Governor and the Secretary to the Treasury, and maintained the responsibility of the Governor for managing the Bank. With minor variations in the number of members, this has been the structure of the Bank's Board since that time.

The *Reserve Bank Act 1959* preserved the original corporate body, under the new name of the Reserve Bank of Australia, to carry on the central banking functions of the Commonwealth Bank, which had evolved over time; other legislation separated the commercial banking and savings banking activities into the newly created Commonwealth Banking Corporation. The *Reserve Bank Act 1959* took effect from 14 January 1960.

There were no major changes in the functions of the Reserve Bank of Australia until the abolition of Exchange Control following the float of the Australian dollar in 1983. There had, however, been a gradual movement to market-oriented methods of implementing monetary policy, away from a system of direct controls on banks, and in the five years following the appointment of a major financial system inquiry (the Campbell Committee, in 1979), it became a fully deregulated system. At the same time, the Reserve Bank of Australia gradually built up a specialised banking supervision function.

Another inquiry into the Australian financial system (the Wallis Committee) was announced in 1996. There were two major outcomes of this inquiry for the Bank, both taking effect from 1 July 1998. The banking supervision function was transferred from the Reserve Bank of Australia to a newly created authority, the Australian Prudential Regulation Authority, which was to be responsible for the supervision of all deposit-taking institutions. The *Reserve Bank Act* was amended also to create a new Payments System Board, with a mandate to promote the safety and efficiency of the Australian payments system. New legislation – the *Payment Systems (Regulation) Act 1998* and the *Payment Systems and Netting Act 1998* – was introduced, giving the Bank relevant powers in this area.

A further inquiry into the Australian financial system was announced by the new Government late in 2013. The terms of reference are broad-ranging, covering aspects such as: the consequences of developments in the Australian financial system since the 1997 inquiry and the global financial crisis; the philosophy, principles and objectives underpinning the development of a well-functioning financial system; and the emerging opportunities and challenges that are likely to drive further change in the global and domestic financial system. The Reserve Bank made a detailed submission to the Financial System Inquiry in March 2014.

The Reserve Bank Board's obligations with respect to the formulation and implementation of monetary policy are laid out in the *Reserve Bank Act*. Section 10(2) of the Act, which is often referred to as the Bank's 'charter', says:
"It is the duty of the Reserve Bank Board, within the limits of its powers, to ensure that the monetary and banking policy of the Bank is directed to the greatest advantage of the people of Australia and that the powers of the Bank ... are exercised in such a manner as, in the opinion of the Reserve Bank Board, will best contribute to:
- the stability of the currency of Australia;
- the maintenance of full employment in Australia; and
- the economic prosperity and welfare of the people of Australia."

**Answer these questions:**

1. What was the purpose of establishing the Commonwealth Bank in 1911? Why wasn't it established earlier? (Think.)

   _____

   _____

2. In 1959 the Reserve Bank of Australia was created. What was it intended to do?

   _____

   _____

3. Do you think that the separating of the Reserve Bank from other banks is a good idea? Explain your answer.

   _____

# Other Forms of Institutions

## Financial Institutions

Financial services are the economic services provided by the finance industry, which encompasses a broad range of businesses that manage money, including credit unions, banks, credit-card companies, insurance companies, accountancy companies, consumer-finance companies, stock brokerages, investment funds and some.

1. **Merchant Banks**: operate primarily in wholesale markets, borrowing from, and lending to, large corporations and government agencies. Other services, including advisory, relate to corporate finance, capital markets, foreign exchange and investment management.

2. **Investment banks**: investment banking is a financial institution that assists individuals, corporations, and governments in raising financial capital by underwriting or acting as the client's agent in the issuance of securities. Their duties include the following:

   a. **Investment management:** the term usually given to describe companies which run collective investment funds. It also refers to services provided by others, generally registered with the Australian Securities and Investment Commission.

   b. **Registered Investment Advisors:** this is an Investment banking financial service focused on creating capital through client investments.

   c. **Hedge Fund Management:** hedge funds often employ the services of " prime brokerage" divisions at major investment banks to execute their trades.

   d. **Custody services**: their job is to look after customers' securities and other assets in electronic or physical form. They process the world's securities trades and service the associated portfolios. Assets under custody in the world are approximately US$100 trillion.

3. **Capital markets services:** underwrite debt and equity, assist company deals (advisory services, underwriting, mergers and acquisitions and advisory fees), and restructure debt into structured finance products.

4. **Private Banking:** Private banks provide banking services exclusively to wealthy individuals. Many financial service firms require a person or family to have a certain minimum net worth to qualify for private banking services. Private banks often provide more personal services, such as wealth management and tax planning, than normal retail banks.

5. **Finance Companies:** provide loans to households and small to medium-sized businesses. Finance companies raise funds from wholesale markets and, using debentures and unsecured notes, from retail investors.

**Answer these questions:**

1. What is the Australian Securities and Investment Commission?

   _____

   _____

2. Explain the following terms:

   a. hedge funds: _____

   _____

   b. underwriting (debt):_____

   _____

   c. equity: _____

   _____

   d. brokerage firm: _____

   _____

   e. debentures: _____

   _____

## Insurers and Fund Managers

1. **Life Insurance Companies:** provide life, accident and disability insurance, annuities, investment and superannuation products. Assets are managed in statutory funds on a fiduciary basis, and are mostly invested in equities and debt securities. Companies will often reinsure, that is part of the amount insured is sold to other insurers to protect them from catastrophic losses.

2. **Insurance underwriting:** Personal lines insurance underwriters actually underwrite insurance for individuals, a service still offered primarily through agents, insurance brokers and stock brokers. Underwriters may also offer similar commercial lines of coverage for businesses. Activities include insurance and annuities, life insurance, retirement insurance, health insurance, property insurance and casualty insurance. Websites have been created to give consumers basic price comparisons for services such as insurance, causing controversy within the industry.

3. **General Insurance Companies:** provide insurance for property, motor vehicles, employers' liability, etc. Assets are invested mainly in deposits and loans, government securities and equities.

4.  **Superannuation and other approved funds:** superannuation funds accept and manage contributions from employers (incl. self-employed) and/or employees to provide retirement income benefits. Funds are controlled by trustees, who often use professional funds managers/advisers. Superannuation funds usually invest in a range of assets (equities, property, debt securities, deposits.

5.  **Cash Management Funds:** unit trusts pool the investors' funds, usually into specific types of assets (e.g., cash, equities, property, money market investments, mortgages, overseas securities). Most unit trusts are managed by subsidiaries of banks, insurance companies or merchant banks.

6.  **Insurance brokerage:** facilitate the buying and selling of financial securities between a buyer and a seller. In today's market, brokerages services are offered online to self-trading investors throughout the world who have the option of trading with 'tied' online trading platforms offered by a banking institution or with online trading platforms sometimes offered in a group by so called online trading portals.

7.  **Friendly Societies**: mutually owned co-operative financial institutions offering benefits to members through a trust-like structure. Benefits include: investment products through insurance or education bonds; funeral; accident; sickness; or other benefits.

**Define the following:**

1.  statutory fund: _____

_____

2.  fiduciary: _____

_____

3.  annuities: _____

_____

4.  Find the name of 4 insurance companies. List the type of insurance they offer. N.B. Insurance companies may specialize rather than cover too many areas.

_____

_____

_____

_____

_____

© Valerie Marett
Coroneos Publications

# Other Financial Services

1.  **Credit Cards:** this has been discussed extensively before. Go back and re-read pages 16-18. **Remember: most debit cards can now be used when credit cards are required and you cannot spend more money than you have.**

    Companies which provide credit card machine and payment networks call themselves "merchant card providers".

2.  **Private Equity Funds:** these funds are typically closed-end funds, which usually take controlling equity stakes in businesses that are either private, or become private once acquired. Private equity funds often use leveraged buyouts to acquire the firms in which they invest. The most successful private equity funds can generate returns significantly higher than that provided by the equity markets, (the market in which ordinary shares are issued or traded).

3.  **Venture Capital:** this is a type of private equity capital typically provided by professional, outside investors to new, high-growth-potential companies in the interest of taking the company to an initial public offering or trade sale of the business.

4.  **Angel investment:** an angel investor or angel (known as a business angel or informal investor in Europe), is an affluent individual who provides capital for a business start-up, usually in exchange for convertible debt or ownership equity. A small but increasing number of angel investors organize themselves into angel groups or angel networks to share resources and pool their investment capital.

5.  **Conglomerates:** a financial services company, such as a universal bank that is active in more than one sector of the financial services market e.g. life insurance, general insurance, health insurance, asset management, retail banking, wholesale banking, investment banking, etc. A key rationale for the existence of such businesses is the existence of diversification benefits that are present when different types of businesses are aggregated, i.e., bad things don't always happen at the same time. As a consequence, economic capital –the amount of money that a firm needs to ensure that the company stays solvent, is usually substantially less for a conglomerate.

6.  **Debt Resolution:** this is a consumer service that assists individuals that have too much debt to pay off as requested, but do not want to file bankruptcy and wish to pay off their debts owed. This debt can be accrued in various ways including but not limited to personal loans, credit cards or in some cases merchant accounts.

    **Financial Counselling** is a free service offered by community organisations, community legal centres and some government agencies. Financial counsellors can help you solve your money problems. Other debt resolution councillors are not free and will charge for services.

7. **Factoring:** factoring is a financial transaction and a type of debtor finance in which a business sells its accounts receivable (i.e., invoices) to a third party (called a *factor*) at a discount. A business will sometimes *factor* its receivable assets to meet its present and immediate cash needs. Banks do this if debts, such as credit cards, are not paid. The factor then peruses the debtor and charges approximately $100 every time they call or write so the amount owed can rise rapidly.

8. **Bankruptcy:** when a person is overwhelmed with debt and has no hope of paying or coming to an agreement with their creditors they may declare bankruptcy. The consequences of bankruptcy are serious and bankruptcy cannot be cancelled if the person changes their mind.

   When a person becomes bankrupt the following occurs:
   - assets, including the house, may be sold
   - income, employment and business may be affected. If income exceeds a certain limit the person may be required to make contributions from their income.
   - they may not be released from all debts
   - the ability to travel overseas will be affected
   - the name of the person declaring bankruptcy will appear on the National Personal Insolvency index for ever
   - the ability to obtain future credit will be affected
   - the bankruptcy will be administered by a trustee
   - bankruptcy will last between 3 and 7 years.
   - the person cannot conceal, remove or dispose of any property inside or outside Australia. If you do, you may be subject to criminal prosecution.

**Answer these questions:**

1. Research and list the top 5 reasons why people become bankrupt.

   _____

   _____

   _____

   _____

2. Of the 5 reasons you have listed, which are the 2 that are likely to affect you most as young adults? Why?

   _____

   _____

3. List 2 places locally you can go for help if you fall into debt.

   _____

   _____

# Shares

People invest in shares with the objective of generating wealth – either through potential share price growth, or via income paid as dividends, or a combination of both. Shares can be bought and sold on the Australian Securities Exchange (ASX). Buying shares has historically given a better chance of making your money grow over a long period than other investments, but with that potential comes a higher risk of losses. Shares are sometimes also known as equities, securities, or stocks.

A person does not need large amounts of money to get started. They can buy as little as $500 worth of shares. As with any investment, shares also carry risk and investors need to inform themselves of these.

## What are shares?
By investing in shares a person is buying part ownership of a company. If the company performs well, the shareholder can benefit from share price growth and/or income paid as dividends. Equally, if the company performs poorly, the shares could decrease in value and/or the company may pay no dividends.

Trades are issued by listed companies and traded by investors on the ASX share-market. A person can trade shares by using a licensed broker to buy and sell shares on their behalf. Shares represent ownership of a company. When an individual buys shares in a company, they become one of its owners. Shareholders choose who runs a company and are involved in making key decisions, such as whether a business should be sold.

While shares are most obviously associated with the stock market, most small businesses are more likely to issue shares in their company in return for a lump sum investment. This investment may either come from friends and family or, for businesses that are looking for capital to fund high growth, through formal equity funding finance.

## Stock Markets
The stock market is the market in which shares of publicly held companies are issued and traded either through exchanges or over-the-counter markets. Investors who use the share market are willing to put up capital for a share in a growth business. The advantage of raising money in this way is that the owner doesn't have to pay the money back or pay interest to the investors. Instead, shareholders are entitled to a share of the distributable profits of the company, known as **dividends**.

Shares can rise in value over time and may be sold for more than the price paid. The difference in the price bought for and the price sold is known as your **capital growth. Capital Gains Tax** is payable on the profit.

## What are the risks?
Shares are considered to be the riskiest way of increasing wealth. The price of

shares can fall as well as rise, which means money can be lost. If a company declares bankruptcy, share holders in the company could lose all the money invested as shareholders are last in the queue to be paid. Larger, more established companies are considered less risky than smaller, start-up companies as they are less likely to go out of business, but it can still happen.

The value of your shares will go up and down from month to month, and the dividend may vary.

**Beware of scams offering you access to exotic or unusual 'investments'. If you've never heard of a type of investment opportunity before there's a good chance it is a scam.**

**Answer these questions;**

1. What are shares? Explain in your own words.

    _____

    _____

2. What is the main Australian share market?

    _____

3. What is the Stock Market?

    _____

4. Define the following:

    a. capital growth: _____

    _____

    b. dividends: _____

    _____

    c. Capital Gains Tax: _____

    _____

5. When you buy shares what are the risks you take?

    _____

6. Find out what are the 5 top performing shares. Write their names below and the price to purchase them.

    _____

    _____

# Superannuation

Superannuation is a way to save for retirement. The money comes from contributions made into the super fund by an employer and, may also be topped up by your own money. Sometimes the government will add to superannuation through co-contributions and the low income super contribution.

An employer must pay 9.5% of the employee's salary into a super fund. This is called the Super Guarantee. The Super Guarantee will gradually increase to 12% in coming years.

Over the course of a person's working life, these contributions from an employer add up, or 'accumulate'. The money is also invested by your super fund so it grows over time. The money that is paid into superannuation funds must generally stay there until the person reaches retirement, or when they begin a transition to retirement, both after a set minimum age. For Australians, in the years to come, super will be their main form of retirement income.

As contributions to your super fund and their earnings are generally taxed at just 15%, this makes super one of the most tax-effective investment vehicles.

## How does superannuation work?
Superannuation is a framework for holding investment assets. It's not an investment in itself. Super funds can offer a range of investment options and asset classes that may include cash, property, shares and fixed interest.

When money is placed into a superannuation fund and an investment option is chosen, a person is actually buying units in these funds. The number of units depends on the daily unit price. This price will vary daily according to changes in the market.

## What are the different types of Superannuation funds?
There are several different types of superannuation funds. The mains ones are;
- **Employer/corporate/staff funds** - these are funds established by an employer for the benefit of their staff.
- **Personal funds** - as the name implies, you personally join as an individual through a super provider. There are many available and most will offer a wide range of investment choices and other features.
- **Industry funds** - these were originally set up for people working in a particular industry, e.g., builders or health care workers. Many are now available to the public.
- **Self-managed super funds** -(also called 'do it yourself' funds) - these can have up to four members and are generally used by people with larger amounts in super or by family groups and are managed by them.

## Withdrawing money from super
Usually, you are restricted from accessing your super money until you reach your preservation age. Your preservation age is based on your date of birth and at present ranges between 55 and 60. It is unlikely you will be able to withdraw your superannuation before you are 65.

**Answer these questions:**

1. Explain simply in your own words what superannuation is.

_____

_____

2. Name the four different types of superannuation funds and explain what each is.

_____

_____

_____

_____

_____

_____

3. What is the present minimum age for withdrawing superannuation?

_____

4. Think! Why do you think successive Governments have made superannuation compulsory?

_____

_____

5. Investigate the range of superannuation funds available. When you obtain a job an employer will register your superannuation in a fund unless you chose one of your own. Below write the name of the fund you consider to be best for you and explain why.

_____

_____

_____

_____

_____

# International Trade

International trade is the buying and selling of goods and services across national borders. It is the backbone of our modern, commercial world, as producers in various nations try to profit from an expanded market, rather than be limited to selling within their own borders. There are many reasons that trade across national borders occurs, including lower production costs in one region versus another, specialized industries, lack or surplus of natural resources and consumer tastes.

International trade accounts for a good part of a country's gross domestic product. It is also one of important sources of revenue for a developing country.

From the earliest times trade has gone on between countries. As far back as the Egyptians  extensive trading was carried out in the Red Sea and with countries around them. The Romans had a vast trading network with the countries they conquered, bringing back trade from the known corners of the world.

The Silk Road was a network of roads that linked trade throughout Asia to  China as far back as the Persian rule in 500 B.C.  The Greeks and Romans also traded with China through these routes, although trade was slow and goods were expensive. By the 1700s fast sailing ships, called Clippers, with special crew, were used to transport tea from China, and spices from Dutch East Indies to different European countries.

Australia's first export was wool and the first shipment to the wool mills in England was in 1807. Within four decades Australia had become the biggest exporter of wool in the world. Although wool is no longer one of our top exports we still export $3 billion of wool around the world.

Australia exports many products including  iron ore and concentrates, coal, natural gas, education, ores, gold, meat, cereals, crude petroleum, beef, aluminum, copper, pharmaceuticals, and medical technical equipment.

Our imports include machines, engines, pumps, vehicles, oil, electronic equipment, pharmaceuticals, iron and steel products, gems and precious metals, furniture and lighting.

Our main two way trade partners are China, Japan, U.S., Republic of Korea, Singapore, New Zealand, U.K., Malaysia, Thailand, Germany, Indonesia, India, Taiwan, Vietnam and the United Arab Emirates.

We trade with other countries because we do not produce some goods and because some goods can be obtained more cheaply from other countries. You have already learnt that the division of labour may help to increase efficiency, expand output and increase Australia's standard of living. In many cases countries may increase their standard of living even further if they specialise in the production of certain goods and purchase others from overseas. This was the reasoning behind getting rid of our electronic industry in the 1970's.

Many companies are now outsourcing services to Asia where labour costs are cheaper. This is because of the law of **comparative costs**, (or the principle of comparative advantages,) which states: a country will gain by specialising in those forms of production in which it has the greater comparative advantage or in which its comparative disadvantage is less. An example of this is that both Australia and U.S. produce cotton and wheat. The U.S. can produce more of both per unit of productive resources: U.S. produces 5 million bales of cotton and 55.4 million tonnes of wheat per year as compared to Australia who produces 2.5 million bales of cotton and 24 million tonnes of wheat. As a result the U.S. has an **absolute** advantage in the production of both and the greater **comparative** advantage.

The greater the freedom of international trade the greater the gains which a country may gain from specialisation according to the theory of comparative advantage. If there are many trade restrictions the gains from specialisation will be less. This international specialisation of particular forms of production is called **Territorial Division of Labour**.

The influence of this on the flow of international trade may be weakened because:

a.  Most trade is conducted without shipping costs and therefore the actual price per unit of productive resources is not the only indicator for judging the differences between countries.

b.  In many countries the Government considers many factors beside comparative advantages when deciding how to use their productive resources, e.g., they may use many resources for defence sources when in many cases these sources could be used more productively elsewhere.

For these reasons it is unlikely that gains from international specialisation will ever be maximized.

**Something to Do:**

Choose two of our two way trade partners. Find out what we export to and import from these countries. Write what you have found below.

_____

_____

_____

_____

_____

_____

# International Payments

Goods bought overseas must be paid for but:

a.  Not only physical goods but services are bought and sold in international trade therefore it would be possible to import physical goods with the aid of earnings received from selling services.

b.  Although total exports must eventually pay for total imports our trade with any one country does not necessarily have to be in balance.

c.  Actual payments in international trade are made through the international connections of our banking system or other similar means of international money transfer.

A simple example of these principles is shown below.

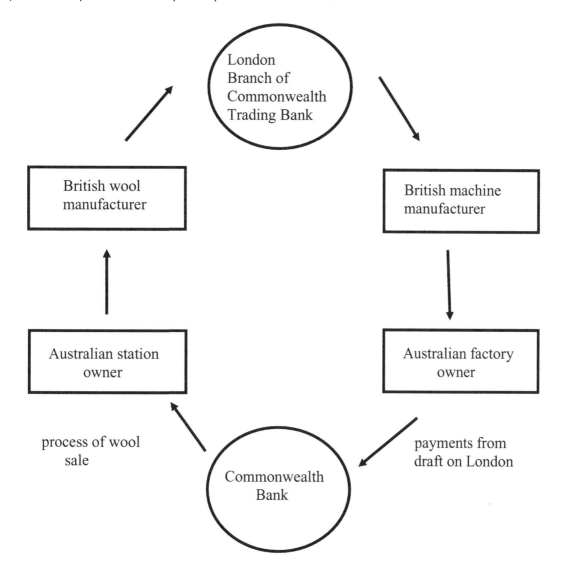

## Balance of Trade

This is the value, over a stated period, of payments received for merchandise exported as compared with the value of payments made for merchandise imported. When we say Australia has a favourable balance of trade we mean payments received from other nations in connection with our export of goods exceeded the payment made to other nations for goods imported.

However in international trade services as well as goods are bought and sold. They are:
- a. insurance, banking charges etc.
- b. payments received for port charges
- c. Australian tourists visiting overseas
- d. Government expenditure, e.g., defence, overseas aid
- e. paying interest to overseas governments and private individuals

Balance of trade therefore refers to the value over a stated period of current payments made internationally for both the visible and invisible items.

## Balance of Payments on Capital Account
This refers to any change in Australian reserves of international currency caused by:
- a. changes in the total of Australian investment abroad
- b. changes in the total overseas investment in Australia

A net capital inflow or net capital outflow may affect or accentuate a surplus or deficit on current accounts. A final surplus or deficit will represent an increase or decrease in Australia's international reserves for the year.

Funds may be invested in Australia from overseas by establishing branches in Australia, purchasing stock or shares in Australia or purchasing properties or businesses.

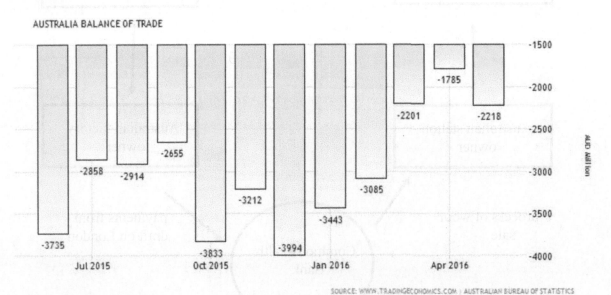

AUSTRALIA BALANCE OF TRADE

SOURCE: WWW.TRADINGECONOMICS.COM | AUSTRALIAN BUREAU OF STATISTICS

Australia reported a trade gap of AUD$2.22 billion in May of 2016, an increase of 24 percent from an upwardly revised AUD$1.79 billion deficit in April and missing market estimates. It was the largest trade deficit since February as exports rose 1.0 percent to AUD$26.17 billion while imports went up 2.0 percent to AUD$28.39 billion. Balance of Trade in Australia averaged -577.63 AUD Million from 1971 until

reaching an all time high of 2241 AUD Million in February of 2009 and a record low of -4358 AUD Million in April of 2015. Balance of Trade in Australia is reported by the Australian Bureau of Statistics.

It is important Australia maintains a necessary level of funds abroad in the banking system to pay for imports. When imports exceed exports it dangerously drains our international reserves.

**Answer these questions:**

1. Define the following terms:

   a. exports: _____

   b. imports: _____

   c. balance of trade: _____

   _____

   d. favourable balance of trade: _____

   _____

2. Give three examples of the international trade services that are bought and sold.

   _____

3. How are funds commonly invested in Australia?

   _____

   _____

## International Monetary Fund
In 1946, in connection with the United Nations Organisation the International Monetary Fund (I.M.F.) and the World Bank was set up. The IMF is an international organization, headquartered in Washington, D.C., of 189 countries with the aim of working to foster global monetary cooperation, secure financial stability, facilitate international trade, promote high employment and sustainable economic growth, and reduce poverty around the world.

## International Lending and Borrowing
For a country to increase its standard of living it must use some productive resource to produce capital goods instead of producing consumer goods. This way a country is saving some national production for the future.

Productive resources: include natural resources, human resources, and capital resources. Natural resources refer to resources such as coal, water, trees, and land itself. Raw materials used in production come from natural resources. Capital resources are goods made and used to produce other goods and services, e.g., include buildings, machinery, tools and equipment.

Increases in productivity allows a given amount of labour to produce a greater amount of output than was possible before the productivity increase. As productivity increases, so do the number of products and markets available. Similarly, as products become less expensive, due to more efficient production methods, the quantity demanded for some of those products also increases. In the long run, increases in productivity are offset by increases in demand, so jobs are not lost.

Australia borrows from overseas countries because quite often the volume of our production is not large enough to satisfy basic needs. By borrowing from overseas countries Australia has been able to purchase capital equipment. This has resulted in a greater increase in the production than would have been possible without borrowing. By borrowing overseas Australia incurs a debt to a foreign country and a liability to meet regular interest payments. Having to pay interest and payments could lower our standard of living unless we make sure we invest the money in industries that would make enough profit and export enough to repay the loan and interest.

If Australia cannot increase its exports sufficiently to cover the interest payments while continuing to borrow, the only alternative is to decrease the current amount of imports.

There are 2 advantages for the lenders of money internationally:
a. The lender can import more goods using interest payments to cover the cost of the additional goods or the lender can use the interest to fund further overseas investments.
b. The country borrowing the money finds further markets for its goods allowing it to maintain or increase its level of production. The level of employment is therefore high and this helps increase the standard of living for the country borrowing the money.

**The International Bank for Reconstruction and Development**
The International Bank for Reconstruction and Development, (IBRD,) was created in 1944 to help Europe rebuild after World War II. Today, IBRD provides loans and other assistance primarily to middle income countries.

IBRD is the original World Bank institution. It works closely with the rest of the World Bank Group to help developing countries reduce poverty, promote economic growth, and build prosperity. It provides a combination of financial resources, knowledge and technical services, and strategic advice to developing countries, including middle income and credit-worthy lower income countries.

**Terms of Trade**
Terms of trade is a term that represents the value of the exports of a country, relative to the value of its imports; the value is calculated by dividing the value of the exports by the imports, with the result then being multiplied by 100. When a country's terms of trade is less than 100% more capital is going out than coming in

When the term of trade is greater than 100%, the country is accumulating more money exports than it is spending. When a country's terms of trade improves, it indicates that for every unit of export that a country sells, it is able to purchase more units of goods that are imported. When a country's terms of trade worsens, it indicates that the country must export a greater number of units in order to purchase the same given number of imports.

## Exchange Rates

Foreign exchange rates state the values of other nation's currencies in terms of our own. Most exchange rates use the US currency as the base currency and the other currency as the counter currency.

There are a few exceptions to this rule, such as the Euro and Commonwealth currencies like the British pound, Australian dollar and New Zealand dollar. Exchange rates for most major currencies are generally expressed to four places after the decimal, except for currency quotations involving the Japanese yen, which are quoted to two places after the decimal.

Exchange rates can be floating or fixed. While floating exchange rates – in which currency rates are determined by market force – are the norm for most major nations, some nations prefer to fix or peg their domestic currencies to a widely accepted currency like the US dollar.

## Balance of Payments

The Australian balance of payment is a systematic record in money terms of all the transactions, which take place over a year, between residents of Australia and all other nations. It encompasses all transactions between a country's residents and its non-residents involving goods, services and income; financial claims on and liabilities to the rest of the world; and transfers such as gifts. The balance of payment is usually calculated every quarter and every calendar year.

If Australian prices rise and Japanese prices remain the same, Australia is in a good place to sell but not to buy.

Originally a country's wealth was based on a gold standard, that is, a nations currency was fixed in terms of its gold, but this broke down in most countries in about 1930. An alternative to fixing a country's exchange rate according to the gold rate is to have a "free rate".

In the retail currency exchange market, different buying and selling rates will be quoted by money dealers. Most trades are to or from the local currency. The buying rate is the rate at which money dealers will buy foreign currency, and the selling rate is the rate at which they will sell that currency. The quoted rates will incorporate an allowance for a dealer's margin (or profit) in trading, or else the margin may be recovered in the form of a commission or in some other way. Different rates may also be quoted for cash (usually notes only), in a documentary form (such as traveller's cheques ) or electronically (such as a credit card purchase).

**Answer these questions:**

1. What is the purpose of the International Monetary Fund?

   _____

   _____

   _____

2. What happens regarding labour when productivity increases?

   _____

   _____

3. How do we ensure that borrowing from overseas does not lower our standard of living?

   _____

   _____

   _____

4. What are the advantages for lenders of money internationally?

   _____

   _____

5. What advantage are there for the borrower to borrow money internationally?

   _____

   _____

6. How does it generally benefit a country when money is borrowed internationally?

   _____

   _____

7. Explain the purpose of the International Bank for Reconstruction and Development.

   _____

   _____

8. How does it fulfil its purpose?

_____

_____

9. Explain the following terms:

a. exchange rates: _____

_____

b. terms of trade: _____

_____

c. balance of payments: _____

_____

10. Most banks show the exchange rate for $1 Australian to:

a. Japanese yen: _____

b. UK pound: _____

c. US dollar: _____

# International Trade Policy

## Terms

**Tariffs:** duties or taxes levied on goods coming into the country.

**Revenue Tariff:** a tax applied to imported and exported goods in order to increase the revenue of a state or federal government.

**Protective Tariff:** a duty imposed on imports to raise their price, making them less attractive to consumers and thus protecting domestic industries from foreign competition.

**Excise Duty:** An excise tax is an indirect tax charged on the sale of a particular good. Excise taxes are considered an indirect form of taxation because the government does not directly apply the tax. An intermediary, either the producer or merchant, is charged and then must pay the tax to the government, e.g., on wine, beer and cigarettes.

**Free Trade Policy:** an international treaty that reduces barriers. It allows better Australian access to important markets; an improved competitive position for Australian exports; more prospects for increased two-way investment, and reduced import costs for Australian businesses and consumers alike.

**Free Trade Policy:** an international treaty that reduces barriers. It allows better Australian access to important markets; an improved competitive position for Australian exports; more prospects for increased two-way investment, and reduced import costs for Australian businesses and consumers alike.

**Protection:** this covers all types of action by the Government to give home producers an advantage over overseas competitors. Protection includes such things as tariffs ands subsidies.

**Exchange Control:** a government restriction on currencies between countries. The Reserve Bank may control the use of the nations reserves and so assist the home producer.

**Import Quotas:** is a physical limit on the quantity of a good that can be produced abroad and that can be imported into a country in a given period of time.

**Embargo:** is an official ban on trade or other commercial activity with a particular country.

**Economic Nationalism:** is a body of policies that emphasize domestic control of the economy, labour and capital formation, even if this requires the imposition of tariffs and other restrictions on the movement of labour, goods and capital.

**Preference Trade Agreements:** is a trading bloc that gives preferential access to certain products from the participating countries. This is done by reducing tariffs but not by abolishing them completely. It can be established through a trade pact.

**Explain the following terms and give at least one example of how these are applied:**

a. tariffs: _____

_____

_____

b. free trade policy: _____

_____

c. embargo: _____

_____

_____

d. excise duty: _____

_____

© Valerie Marett
Coroneos Publications

Australian Homeschooling #564
Basic Economics

e. preference trade agreement: _____

_____

f. protective tariff: _____

_____

g. exchange control: _____

_____

h. revenue tariff: _____

_____

i. protection: _____

_____

j. import quotas: _____

_____

k. economic nationalism: _____

_____

## Australian Trade Policy

**Before Federation**

Prior to Federation, each state decided its own trade policy. Their policies varied from free trade by N.S.W. to the protection policy of Victoria.

**Tariff Board**

The Tariff Board was established in 1921. It consisted of four members, one member being an Administrative Officer of the Department of Trade and Customs. Its main responsibility was to advise the Government on questions of assistance to Australian industries. In particular:

a. whether other forms of protection were desirable
b. the necessity for new duties and whether existing duties should be reduced or increased
c. whether manufacturers were exploiting the public under the protection of tariffs
d. proposals for new tariff agreements from other countries

It was intended the Board would answer broad questions of policy and its economic effects: questions of costs and efficiency as compared with those overseas; retail prices; effects of additional protection.

The 1927 Tariff Enquiry decided that most tariffs could be reduced or abolished and tariffs should be used solely for protection.

## Tariff Policy in the Depression

As a result of the slump in export prices, which occurred in 1929, it was decided that there would have to be large tariff increases since there was a serious deficit in Australia's balance of trade due to the decrease in export prices. As the Depression became more serious, some imports were prohibited altogether in an effort to stimulate Australian industries. Thus a policy of increased tariffs was used as a means of expanding existing industry and promoting new ones in an attempt to increase employment. The disadvantage of this system was that it was likely to lead to retaliation by other countries. It also meant Australian goods would become more expensive. Special rates were worked out with Britain and Commonwealth countries.

High tariffs at the beginning of the Depression did create employment in Australian industries. Australia aimed at self-sufficiency and to achieve this the Government subsidised most forms of primary production except wool.

After the Depression high duties on secondary products were reduced by the Tariff Board and by 1939 Australian tariffs were divided into three main categories:
  a. British preferential tariff: this was the lowest scale of tariff.

  b. Intermediate tariff: applied to countries with whom Australia had trade treaties.

  c. General tariff: merchandise from all other countries.

# Post War Development

After World War II most nations showed a desire for freer world trade. However the aim of achievements in this direction have been agreements between individual nations and groups of nations concerning reductions on tariffs on each other's products.

### British Commonwealth Agreement

### 1932
The members of the British Commonwealth agreed at the Ottawa Conference to give preferential treatment to other Commonwealth countries. At this stage the main Commonwealth countries were Britain, Australia, New Zealand, Canada, South Africa and India. Tariffs on merchandise from foreign countries was raised.

### 1957
An agreement was signed with Britain that modified the Ottawa agreement due to changing world conditions. The margin of tariffs between Commonwealth and foreign countries was lowered.

Later that year an agreement was signed with Japan. Tariffs were to be lowered slightly, especially on sugar, and some two-way trade was to begin.

**Answer these questions:**

1. What happened prior to Federation regarding trade policy? Why did this happen? Would this have been very practical or not? Explain your answer.

_____

_____

_____

_____

_____

_____

2. When was the first tariff board established? What were its duties?

_____

_____

_____

_____

_____

3. How did the Depression affect tariffs?

_____

_____

_____

4. List the 3 main categories of tariffs by 1939.

_____

_____

_____

_____

## After 1957

There has been a gradual decline on the importance of the tariff as a means of protecting Australia. Australia is moving towards a free trade agreement with many countries, although not on all imports or exports. We will look at one of these.

## Japan

Australia and Japan have a long history of trade going back as far as the nineteenth century. Coal was the first recorded traded commodity from Australia to Japan in 1865.

Through the 1950's Australia's economy rode on the sheep's back but it relied heavily on Britain as its primary export market. At the start of the 1950's Japan ranked as Australia's fourth largest export market, but rose to be its second largest export market by 1956. At this time Australia imposed import licensing measures on Japan as well as tariffs and the growing deficit on Japanese products annoyed Japan.

In 1957 after extensive trade talks it was agreed that Australian exports would receive the same treatment as other foreign buyers and in return Japan would be granted the same licensing and export terms accorded to all foreign goods imported into Australia. Japan was no longer to be singled out for specially restrictive measures.

As the United Kingdom's dominance as Australia's trading partner began to wane due to its growing trade with Europe in the 1960's due to its increase trade with Europe, Japan's importance grew. During the 1960's Australia's main exports to Japan were wool, wheat and dairy products and these increased as the United Kingdom established markets in Europe and finally joined the European Common Market in 1972.

At the same time Japan assumed global status as a major industrial power and this created a demand for raw materials. This expansion of Japan into heavy industries such as steel, chemicals, automobiles and shipbuilding proved a boon for Australia's mineral sector and strengthened the well established trade between the two countries.

During the 1970's Japan consolidated its position as Australia's major trading partner. By the middle of 1977-8 Japan took 32.3% of Australia's total exports. During this period there was also a change in goods imported by Australia. Telecommunication, recording and reproducing apparatus and equipment became the second most important export from Japan to Australia and its share of the market was 15.7%.

Until the early 1980's, the Australian Government followed a policy that focused on protecting its domestic industries and maintaining existing levels of market access in Japan. During the 1980s, however, Australia began to pursue a trade policy that strongly advocated an 'open international trade and payments system' and 'an equitable framework of rules based on the principles of multilateralism, non-discrimination, predictability and transparency'. The new approach called for progressive trade liberalisation. Australia looked to promote fair and predictable access to major markets, to place restraints on subsidised competition in third markets and to encourage stability in commodity markets.

The share of Australian exports destined for Japan as a percentage of total Australian exports declined from its peak of over 35% in 1976 to 26% in 1983. Over the same period, Australia's penetration of the Japanese market also declined steadily from more than 8% in the mid-1970s to 5% in 1984. In part, Australia was losing its share of a growing Japanese market because of changes in Japan's economic structure and changes in its demand for imports.

After a minerals led investment boom in the early 1980s, export of energy minerals to Japan grew rapidly, especially coal but also including oil and gas which began to assume a prominent role in Australia's exports. Trade in services between the two countries increased markedly during the 1980s, especially in the areas of financial services and tourism.

During the 1980s, the level of Japanese foreign investment in Australia increased substantially. In 1980–81, the amount stood at just over $4 billion; by 1985–86, it had more than quadrupled to over $20 billion. Nonetheless, the United States and the United Kingdom were by far the most important foreign investors in Australia during the mid-1980s.

Towards the end of the decade the substantial purchases of real estate by Japanese companies stirred anti-Japanese feelings in some sectors of the Australian community. Throughout the late 1980s and into the early years of the 1990s, Japanese investors turned to the tourist industry and real estate as their main targets for investment. This very public foreign investment provoked some Australians to question the economic benefits that it would bring to the local community.

While Japan's direct investment in resources, automobile manufacturing and tourism was widely recognised in Australia, Australia's investment in Japan was minuscule.

At the beginning of the 1990s, Japan stood as the leading nation among Australia's export partners and one of the most important sources of Australia's imports. The economies of both countries had grown considerably since the war and their relationship had matured into a friendly and mutually beneficial partnership. However, as Japan's economic troubles deepened in the 1990s, many economists in Australia feared that Australia's trading prospects would suffer. Since 1990, when Japan entered a prolonged period of sluggish economic activity, its dominance as an export destination for Australian products and as a supplier of goods to Australia has been eroded. Even so, Australia's export trade to Japan has held up well to date and Japan still retains its position as Australia's single largest export market.

Even though Australia's trade with Japan over the decades has diversified, it nonetheless is built around a tight cluster of core commodities. Throughout the 1990s, Australia remained heavily dependent on mineral and agricultural exports. Five commodities, all from primary industry, accounted for over half of Australian exports of $16 billion in 1994—coal, beef, gold, iron ore and natural gas. In 1996, the export of non-monetary gold to Japan fell sharply and has not recovered. In 1997–98, Japan accounted for around 17% of agricultural, 17% of mineral and 42% of energy exports from Australia. The total value was in excess of $8 billion dollars.

The Japan-Australia Economic Partnership Agreement (JAEPA) entered into force on 15 January 2015. The Agreement provides valuable preferential access for

Australia's exports will support further growth in two-way investment. JAEPA is by far the most liberalising trade agreement Japan has ever concluded. It provides Australian exporters, importers, investors and producers a significant advantage over their international competitors.

The Japan-Australia Economic Partnership Agreement (JAEPA) delivers substantial benefits for the Australian economy, making it easier to do business with Japan, our 2nd largest trading partner. The Agreement will strengthen and deepen trade between two of the Asia-Pacific's largest economies.

**Answer these questions:**

1. Outline trade between Australia and Japan from the beginning to a free trade agreement.

_____

_____

_____

_____

_____

_____

_____

_____

_____

_____

_____

_____

_____

_____

_____

_____

_____

_____

_____

_____

_____

_____

_____

2. Research and outline a history with China as a trading partner up to the free trade agreement made on 20th December 2015. (Use a separate sheet of paper.)

# Free Trade Policy Compared with Protection Policy

Arguments for and against protectionism can be summed up as follows:

## Arguments for Protectionism
- Protection against cheap foreign labour
- National defence
- Preservation of particular classes or occupations in the population
- Infant industries
- Real wages and protection of employment
- Balance of payments
- A more balanced and self-sufficient economy

## Arguments against protectionism
- Protection taxes exporters
- Net loss of income
- Loss of employment
- Reducing protection improves productivity
- Greater opportunities for exports of goods and services

If we give too much protection to industry and the wrong form of protectionism we promote inefficiency, increased costs and prices and sacrifice the real benefits of international trade.

For an economy to reach maturity it must be balanced, where secondary industries are as important as primary industries. Protectionism helps an economy when the protection is used to foster potentially efficient infant industries. This gives them a chance to grow and develop without having to compete with overseas companies that are cheaper. If however there is no chance of the infant industry ever running efficiently, the tariffs on overseas goods become a burden on the economy. Protectionism should be confined to those industries that need it least.

Since the depression years many uneconomic industries have been fostered and many substitute products have been developed at a considerable cost. In many cases this tariff policy was adopted for uneconomic reasons, namely the threat of war and therefore the need to obtain the security of economic self-sufficiency.

The economists' test of protectionism should be to consider the effect on real income per head of population and the size of the population which can be supported. That is, can more goods and services be provided for more people?

## Research and Write

Research why Australia's first trade policies were protectionist and why she is now leaning more and more towards free trade policies. Include the pros and cons of both and conclude with your opinion on how far Australia should go in allowing purchases of Australian businesses and real estate.

# Public Finance

## Government Aims:
- to maintain a stable rate of growth
- to have an equal distribution of income
- to maintain employment

## Sources of Revenue
- loans
- taxes
  - a. direct taxes through income tax etc.
  - b. indirect tax through sales tax, GST etc.

There are as many as 160 different state taxes and 259 taxes nationally. Most Australians pay 125 different taxes a year.

## Expenditure, State and Federal

Most modern governments have assumed responsibilities for regulating their economies to assist in certain desirable ends. The most important of these are:
- to maintain full employment
- a fair and reasonable distribution of income between the members of a community
- a stable rate of growth in the economy

The maintenance of full employment is considered to be the responsibility of the Federal Government.

To maintain their functions the government—federal, state or local—is involved in heavy expenditure in many directions. The Budget has a significant role to play in the carrying out of government aims with a view to creating conditions which promote economic growth.

This situation may be contrasted with nineteenth century England where the annual budget had a minor role to play in the economy. In this period it was often argued that the most efficient economic system was one in which the government refrained from interfering and therefore annual budgets were framed along the following lines:
- government expenditure should be as low as possible, therefore government responsibilities were strictly limited
- the budget should be balanced, that is, revenue should pay all expenditure, which would mean the government would play a neutral role and not upset the balance of the economy
- taxes should be designed so as to have as little effect as possible on human behaviour and on the working of the economic system.

Nineteenth century government was against goods and services tax as it altered human behaviour. They were also against progressive income tax because this would hit the capitalists. The tax they agreed upon was proportional income tax.

In the twentieth and twenty first century, and especially since 1939, the Budget has assumed a more and more significant role in the economy. Few economists accept the view that the economic forces of the market necessarily promote the best economic interests of the community. The modern view is that the government is able to improve the economic system and therefore should play a role.

The government changed its opinion because of:
- the need for social services
- changes in economic circumstances
- the use of the gross domestic product. The gross domestic product (GDP) is one of the primary indicators used to gauge the health of a country's economy. It represents the total dollar value of all goods and services produced over a specific time period.
- developments in the field of economic theory

This meant:
- low government expenditure is not necessarily a good thing
- the budget is constructed according to the current economic situation
- taxes are designed to help the economy in various ways.

**Answer these questions:**

1. What are the aims of a modern government in regard to finances?

   _____

   _____

   _____

2. How do governments find the revenue to finance their aims?

   _____

   _____

3. Outline the views held by government in the nineteenth century.

   _____

   _____

   _____

   _____

   _____

   _____

4. What is meant by a "balanced budget?"

   _____

   _____

© Valerie Marett
Coroneos Publications

Australian Homeschooling #564
Basic Economics

5. Why did government change its opinion about the role government should play?

_____

_____

_____

_____

_____

6. How did these changes in opinion change the government's Budget?

_____

_____

_____

**Think and discuss the following questions with your parents before answering them.**

7. Is it really a government's responsibility to redistribute income? Does this really work? Explain your answer.

_____

_____

_____

_____

_____

_____

8. Australia's welfare bill is $140-190 billion a year. 8 out of 10 Australians work to pay this bill. This includes all forms of government handouts. While we should help those in genuine need can we really afford this? What is the obvious solution?

_____

_____

_____

9. Do we expect too much from our governments? Explain.

_____

_____

# Federal and State Government Expenditure

## Federal Government

During World War II the Federal Government expenditure greatly increased, although after reaching an increased spending expenditure during World War II there was a steady decline until 1947-8. Since 1950-1 expenditure has exceeded the peak of the War years.

## Why?

Prior to this time **classical economic** thinking held that markets function best with minimal government interference. Cyclical swings in employment and economic output would be modest and self-adjusting. According to this classical theory, if aggregate demand fell, or the total demand for goods and services in an economy at a given time fell, the resulting weakness in production and jobs would lead to a decline in prices and wages. A lower level of inflation and wages would induce employers to make capital investments and employ more people, stimulating employment and restoring economic growth.

The depth and severity of the Great Depression, however, severely tested this hypothesis. A man called **John Maynard Keynes** published a book in 1936 called the "General Theory of Employment." Keynes said capitalism was a good economic system. In a capitalist system, people earn money from their work. Businesses employ and pay people to work. Then people can spend their money on things they want. Other people work and make things to buy. Sometimes the capitalist system has problems. People lose their work. Businesses close. People cannot work and cannot spend money. Keynes said then the government should step in and help people who do not have work.

This idea is called "**demand-side policy**". If people are working, the economy is good. If people are not working, the economy is bad. Keynes said when the economy is bad, people want to save their money. That is, they do not spend their money on things they want. As a result, there is less economic activity.

He said the government should spend more money when people do not have work. The government can borrow money and give people jobs (work). Then people can spend money again and buy things. This helps other people find work.

Some people, such as **conservatives, libertarians** and people who believe in **Austrian economics** do not agree with Keynes' ideas. They say government work does not help capitalism. They say when the government borrows money, it takes money away from businesses. They do not like Keynesian economics because they say the economy can get better without government help.

During the late 1970s, Keynesian economics became less popular because inflation was high at the same time that unemployment was high. This is because many people interpreted Keynesian theory to say that it was impossible for there to be both high inflation and high unemployment.

Keynes ideas:
- The market for goods controls employment and production. The market for work does not.
- It is possible that people become unemployed even if they want to work.
- An increase in savings will not lead to an increase in investment the same amount. People have the choice between investing their money or saving it.
- An economic system based on money is different from one that is based on the exchange of goods.
- The quantity theory of money is only valid if there is no unemployment. The quantity theory of money states that money supply has a direct, proportional relationship with the price level. For example, if the currency in circulation increased, there would be a proportional increase in the price of goods.
- In a market economy, investor behavior is governed by what Keynes called the "animal spirits" of investors, that is the human emotion that drives human confidence.

From 1958-9 the Federal Government greatly increased expenditure because:
- there were more people therefore more public works and services were needed
- great increase in war and repatriation expenditure
- more social services obligations
- the payments to the states increased due to the Federal Government taking over income tax
- there was a great increase in prices

2007-2009 there was a Global Financial Crisis (GFC). The GFC was followed by the deepest recession in the world economy since World War II. The Keynesian economics became more popular. Leaders around the world created stimulus packages which would allow their government to spend a lot of money to create jobs.

The Australian economy performed better during this period than other advanced economies on nearly all relevant indicators. Financial conditions were stressed, but the financial system held up remarkably well; the economy slowed, but did not fall into recession; and while unemployment rose, it did so by far less than in many other advanced economies. The crisis had a substantial impact on the solvency and liquidity of a significant number of financial institutions globally, causing share prices of banks to fall sharply, and some major financial institutions to collapse. The weaker global economy also resulted in a reduction in demand for Australia's exports, with subsequent falls in Australia's terms of trade.

The Australian economy slowed, but the slowdown was much more moderate than in most other advanced countries and the economy recovered more quickly. Confidence recovered faster in Australia than in other OECD countries. Business confidence started to recover from February 2009, following the announcement of the Nation Building and Jobs Plan and a further cut in the official cash rate. Consumer confidence rebounded sharply in June 2009 following the announcement of the March quarter 2009 GDP outcome, where the economy recorded solid positive growth, avoiding two consecutive quarters of falling real GDP.

Australia's resilience during the global downturn has been attributed to a range of factors. There is considerable disagreement about the extent to which the different factors, either individually or collectively, were important.

A key factor underpinning the resilience of the Australian economy during this episode was the resilience of the Australian financial system. Australia's financial system was appropriately regulated and well supervised in the lead-up to the crisis, and the underlying strength of the system was buttressed at a key time by both the Reserve Bank of Australia and the Government. In sharp contrast with many other advanced economies, no major Australian bank failed during the financial crisis. Australian banks remained profitable, and were able to access capital markets, enabling them to continue to lend.

The Government put in place a range of other measures to support the financial sector, including providing government guarantees for deposits and for wholesale debt securities issued by ADIs, and directing the purchase by the AOFM of a substantial package of mortgage-backed securities. This supported the continued flow of credit to the economy, avoiding a potentially damaging credit squeeze. A key reason for the strong position of the Australian financial system entering the crisis was the effectiveness of financial regulations and regulators in the lead up to the crisis.

The Reserve Bank of Australia eased monetary policy significantly in response to the global downturn, with the official cash rate falling from 7.25 per cent at the start of September 2008 to 3 per cent in April 2009.

The sharp fall in the Australian dollar also helped. The fall in the currency was partly due to the sharp reduction in Australian official interest rates.

In October 2008 the Government announced a $10.4 billion fiscal stimulus package in its *Economic Security Strategy*, largely comprising cash transfers to low and middle income earners. In November 2008 the Government announced a $15.2 billion COAG funding package, with funds to be delivered over a five-year period, including a substantial amount in the first half of 2009. A further $4.7 billion stimulus was announced in the December 2008 Nation Building package. The $42 billion *Nation Building and Jobs Plan* announced in February 2009 included payments to low and middle income earners and investment in schools, housing, energy efficiency, community infrastructure, roads and support for small businesses.

There has been much debate as to whether or not this fiscal stimulus helped. Certainly the payment of more than $900 to each Australian adult, weakened the Treasury, but did little over all to help the economy as many people saved the money rather than spending it.

Several Labor Governments took Australia from a surplus to a deficit, from which Australia has still not recovered. The table on the next page shows areas of Federal Government expenditure and the cost of each.

| | Estimates | | | Projections | |
|---|---|---|---|---|---|
| | 2015-16 | 2016-17 | 2017-18 | 2018-19 | 2019-20 |
| | $m | $m | $m | $m | $m |
| General public services | 23,967 | 22,659 | 21,790 | 22,345 | 23,537 |
| Defence | 25,986 | 27,155 | 27,937 | 29,384 | 31,525 |
| Public order and safety | 4,958 | 4,915 | 4,766 | 4,719 | 4,675 |
| Education | 32,515 | 33,669 | 33,815 | 34,494 | 35,804 |
| Health | 69,172 | 71,413 | 73,425 | 76,239 | 79,260 |
| Social security and welfare | 152,838 | 158,612 | 166,518 | 184,260 | 191,828 |
| Housing and community amenities | 4,865 | 5,282 | 5,051 | 4,455 | 4,412 |
| Recreation and culture | 3,512 | 3,401 | 3,337 | 3,249 | 3,301 |
| Fuel and energy | 6,528 | 6,687 | 6,782 | 7,028 | 7,301 |
| Agriculture, forestry and fishing | 2,768 | 3,122 | 3,084 | 2,626 | 2,269 |
| Mining, manufacturing and construction | 3,650 | 3,545 | 3,792 | 3,999 | 4,277 |
| Transport and communication | 8,647 | 11,131 | 10,606 | 6,599 | 5,400 |
| Other economic affairs | 9,626 | 9,832 | 8,620 | 8,600 | 8,531 |
| Other purposes | 82,437 | 89,129 | 95,291 | 101,326 | 109,483 |
| Total expenses | 431,470 | 450,553 | 464,812 | 489,324 | 511,604 |

## State & Territory Governments

There has been an ever growing increase in state government expenditure but less rapidly increasing revenue.

State Governments are responsible for:
- agriculture
- education
- electricity and gas supplies
- health
- housing
- law and order
- local government
- main roads
- police
- public transport
- water supply

State Governments receive shares of the GST and financial aid for education, health, and work projects. They collect payroll tax, sales tax and taxes on motor vehicles.

## Answer these questions:

1. Explain the following economic theories. You may use a dictionary or the internet if you need to, to simplify your answers.

a. **classical economics :** _____

_____

b.  **Keynesian economics:** _____

_____

c.  **demand-side policy:** _____

_____

d.  **conservativism:** _____

_____

e.  **libertarianism:** _____

_____

f.  **Austrian economics:** _____

_____

2.  What was the GFC? Who did this affect?

_____

_____

3.  Briefly list the attempts Australia made to deal with the GFC.

_____

_____

_____

_____

_____

_____

_____

_____

_____

_____

_____

4.  Did the Government's stimulus efforts help? Explain your answer. (You will need to do some research.)

_____

_____

_____

# Taxation

## Direct Taxation

These are taxes on income or capital.

- **Taxable income** is generally on a person's total assessable income less any allowable deductions. If a loss is incurred it may be possible to carry it forward to future years. Assessable income includes items such as salaries, wages, income from business, interest, rent and dividends. Deductions generally include expenses that have been incurred in the course of gaining or producing income.

- **Capital gains tax** is imposed on any gains from assets, e.g., sale of a house under a specified period.

- **Fringe Benefit Tax** (FBT) is imposed on the value of non-cash benefits provided by employers to employees. Generally, benefits must be connected to the employee's employment in order to be taxable, although certain fringe benefits are either specifically subject to FBT or expressly excluded under Australian law. FBT is levied on the provider of the benefit at a flat rate of 46.5% and may be deductible against the employer's taxable income.

- **Medicare Levy and Medicare Levy Surcharge:** Medicare is Australia's public health insurance scheme. It operates by receiving contributions through the Medicare Levy and the Medicare Levy Surcharge, which are taxes imposed on Australian residents' taxable incomes. The Medicare Levy is imposed at a flat rate of 1.5% of an individual's taxable income. The Medicare Levy Surcharge is an additional flat rate of between 1-1.5% imposed on high income earners who do not have private hospital insurance.

- **Superannuation tax – the Superannuation Guarantee Charge:** every employer must pay a minimum level of superannuation (known as the superannuation guarantee) to its employees to ensure that workers have money set aside for their retirement.

## Reasons for Direct Taxation

- equality: everyone with any income contributes to provision of services
- certainty: the tax payer knows how much he has to pay and can allow for it in his budget
- economy: direct taxes are easy to collect
- convenience: it is easier for the tax payer to pay weekly than in one large sum at the end at the end of the year.

## Indirect Taxation

- **Goods and services tax** (GST) is a broad-based tax of 10% on most goods, services and other items sold or consumed in Australia.

- **Luxury car tax:** The luxury car tax is a flat rate of 33% imposed when a luxury car is sold or imported into Australia.

- **Fuel taxes** apply to fuels used in Australia. Fuel taxes raise the most revenue of the taxes levied on goods and services by the Australian Government with the exception of GST. Products subject to fuel taxes include petrol, diesel, certain oils and lubricants, and stabilised crude petroleum oil.

- **Alcohol taxes:** rates of taxation varying considerably for different types of alcoholic beverages. This reflects policy changes over time to meet multiple objectives — raising revenue, reducing the social costs of excessive alcohol consumption, and supporting wine producers and independent beer producers.
- **Tobacco tax:** Taxes on tobacco are the second largest, in terms of revenue raised, of the indirect taxes (excluding GST) raised by the Australian Government. Tobacco taxes raised $8.5 billion in 2013-14.
- **Agricultural levies:** The Australian Government collects agricultural levies at the request of primary producer associations. The purpose of the levies is to provide a significant, reliable and ongoing source of pooled funds for research, development and marketing of particular agricultural commodities.
- **Tariffs:** Tariffs are taxes applied to goods imported into Australia. In 2013-14, revenue was $3.0 billion. Tariffs are usually imposed in order to protect domestic industries, rather than to raise revenue. In general, zero tariffs are expected to lead to higher living standards, regardless of tariffs imposed on Australian goods exported to other countries.

## Advantages of Indirect Taxation
- any rises are often not noticed by the public
- it is easy to increase the tax in an emergency
- taxes are harder to avoid

## Disadvantages of Indirect Tax
- they are regressive, that is the bulk of the taxes come from the poor
- it discriminates unjustly, e.g., beer drinkers and smokers have to pay a heavy tax
- it is inelastic, that is, an increase in tax is not always followed by an increase in revenue

## Answer these questions:

1. Define the following:

   a. taxable income: _____

   _____

   b. capital gains tax: _____

   _____

   c. superannuation tax: _____

   _____

   d. fringe benefits tax: _____

   _____

e. Medicare Levy and Surcharge: _____

_____

f. goods and service tax: _____

_____

g. tobacco tax: _____

_____

h. fuel tax: _____

_____

g. tariffs: _____

_____

h. luxury cars: _____

_____

i. agricultural levy: _____

_____

j. alcohol taxes: _____

_____

2. What do you think are the advantages of indirect tax over direct tax?

_____

_____

_____

_____

3. Australians pay on average 150 taxes levied by Federal and State Governments. Do you think we pay too much tax? Explain your answer. Lower taxes would generally mean less services. Which important services should we keep and which should we get rid of to reduce taxes?

_____

_____

_____

_____

_____

_____

© Valerie Marett
Coroneos Publications

Australian Homeschooling #564
Basic Economics

# Australian Public Debt

To understand Australia's debt you need to understand the following terms:

## Australian Government debt

The Australian Government debt is the amount owed by the Australian Federal Government. The Australian Office of Financial Management, which is part of the Treasury Portfolio, is the agency which manages the government debt and does all the borrowing on behalf of the Australian Government.

## Deficit

A deficit is the amount by which something, especially money, is too small. In terms of the Government, either Federal or State, it means spending more money than they have received in revenue. Money must therefore be borrowed to cover the shortfall.

## Surplus

A surplus is the amount of money left over when all Government expenditure has been met.

## Debt ceiling

A debt ceiling on how much the Australian Government could borrow was created in 2007 by the Rudd Government and set at $75 billion. It was increased in 2009 to $200 billion, $250 billion in 2011, $300 billion in 2012 and $406 billion in 2016.

## Interest

Interest is money paid regularly for the use of the money lent. In 2016 the Government interest **per month** is over 1 million dollars.

## Net Debt

The net debt is the sum of all liabilities (gross debt) of an organisation, less their respective financial assets (cash and other liquid assets). Net debt is one of numerous economic indicators which provide a quantitative measure of the financial health of an organisation.

## Fiscal balance

Fiscal Balance is the difference between revenues and expenditures. A negative fiscal balance implies that expenditures are larger than revenues. In this situation, an organisation is in deficit and will need to borrow money to make up the shortfall in revenues. If the fiscal balance is positive, the organisation is in surplus, which it can then save, give back to its shareholders or use to retire debt.

## Australian National Debt

The term "budget deficit" is most commonly used to refer to government spending rather than business or individual spending. When referring to accrued federal government deficits, the term "national debt" is used.

A budget surplus is a situation in which income exceeds expenditures. The term "budget surplus" is most commonly used to refer to the financial situations of governments; individuals speak of "savings" rather than a "budget surplus." A surplus is considered a sign that government is being run efficiently. A budget surplus might be used to pay off debt, save for the future, or to make a desired purchase that has been delayed, e.g., defence spending.

The public expectations of Government have changed dramatically over the last 60 years. Individual households have come to expect higher levels of living and are not as self-sufficient as previous generations of Australians. The voting public has come to expect increasing levels of government handouts in the form of health, pensions, child care rebates, education etc. (See page 92) More than half the voting population rely on Government handouts, including bureaucrats. These all require Government spending. During the mining boom the Government ran a surplus so there was money available to pay for these expectations, but the money is no longer available. All economies face "boom and bust periods and it is the Government's responsibility to prepare for it.

We have an ever growing number of bureaucrats all dependent on the public purse. Any scheme run by Government requires bureaucrats to administer it. Taking money in tax only to give it back in benefits is inefficient. It would be far better to give tax deductions, which would not require taking the money in the first place, and would therefore require less bureaucracy. Bureaucrats are heavy backers of unions so this would be resisted.

To try and stimulate the economy the Reserve Bank has cut the interest rate several times. This is line with interest rates across the world. Businesses do not however have the confidence to expand and due to high wages unemployment is not falling.

A blowout has occurred as the cost of federal spending programs overwhelms tax revenue. Moody's has issued a veiled warning to the Turnbull Government that Canberra could lose its coveted AAA credit rating, suggesting the steady deterioration in the government's finances has left Australia vulnerable to unforeseen economic shocks, including a collapse in house prices.

The agency noted public debt in Australia had more than tripled in a decade to 35.6 per cent of GDP. Moody's said significant increases in education, health and social security spending had repeatedly caused federal spending to overshoot budget targets. Should Australia lose her AAA rating she will find it harder to obtain further loans and any loans obtained will be at a higher rate of interest. Also countries will be more hesitant to invest in Australia than previously.

However, the ability to borrow that is implicit in government debts enables a country and its government to adjust its actual level of spending below or above the level of money available from taxation and other resources. Thus in case of economic down turn the government can borrow money and spend more money to give a boost to the economy. The money thus borrowed can be repaid in periods of boom when the country may find it convenient or even preferable to cut down its spending below the amount available through taxation.

The major advantage of having government debt is that it allows the government to do more things than it otherwise could. This is similar to how borrowing money to buy a house allows a person to do more things. If government uses its debt wisely, (by investing), this is fine.

A second advantage is that it allows government to be flexible in fiscal policy. If a government has no debt, it has no way to stimulate the economy during a recession. It will also have no credit rating.

The bad thing about government debt is that nobody really pays attention to whether it will earn back more than it cost, in which case it's a hidden or delayed tax to support current governmental decadence. Few private banks would lend private corporations money if their business plan was to build bridges to nowhere.

Too much government borrowing can cause economic problems by driving interest rates up and causing inflation. It is also unwise to run a large deficit to finance spending that is unlikely to cause higher future economic growth. When the national debt to GDP ratio reaches a critical level, investors generally begin to demand higher interest rates due to the higher risk, causing more income to go towards repaying the debt and less towards growth and government services.

Major revenue sources in Australia are in trouble because our national income derived from wages, profits and exports is weak. For individuals, this is experienced as pressure on living standards, while for business it is weak profits, which translate to low levels of investment.

Trying to extract more tax from individuals or businesses simply makes the situation worse. Both sides of politics can feel virtuous about lifting tobacco taxation to raise an additional $3bn a year, but that money is coming out of the pockets of predominantly low-income people whose standards of living are already squeezed. You can't achieve an appreciable lift in tax revenue while national income is flat without hitting growth, investment and living standards.

The only solution is to make an effort to control spending, and at present no politician is willing to do that.

**Answer these questions:**

1. Define the following:

   a. debt ceiling: _____

   _____

   b. net debt: _____

   _____

c. deficit: _____

_____

d. fiscal balance:_____

_____

e. surplus: _____

_____

f. interest: _____

_____

g. national debt: _____

_____

2. Discuss whether or not Australia should reduce and eventually get rid of its deficit. Explain your reason and possible solutions to the problem of reducing debt or if you feel a deficit is not a problem, the outcome for continuing in deficit

_____

_____

_____

_____

_____

_____

_____

_____

_____

_____

_____

_____

_____

_____

_____

© Valerie Marett
Coroneos Publications

Australian Homeschooling #564
Basic Economics

# Basic Economics Answers

1. —Traditional or unplanned economy: individuals produce and market any goods they consider profitable.
—Command economy: a large part of the economy is controlled by a central-ised power.
—Market Economic system: organisa-tions run by the people determine how the economy is run, how supply is generated, what demands are neces-sary etc.
—Mixed economy: This includes capital-ism and socialism. In capitalism the market economic system is largely used but the government regulates fair trade, government programmes, moral business, monopolies, essential services etc.
In socialism the government controls and owns the most profitable and vital industries, but allows the rest of the market to operate freely.

2. Australia is a mixed economy. The government regulates certain industries and services for the good of the people and capitalism prevails in the rest of the society, that is a system based on private ownership of the means of production and their operation for prof-it, e.g., private property ownership, capital accumulation, wages, a price system, and competitive markets.

## Page 28

1. It means that dividing labour into differ-ent processes allows workers to focus on specific tasks.

2. Answers will vary.

3. dependent    necessities    luxuries

4. primary that includes farming, fishing, forestry and mining
secondary which covers processing industries
tertiary which covers services, building industry, shops and entertainment

5. Answers may vary slightly.
With the development of secondary industry in metropolitan and regional areas more jobs are available. As cities grew there was more opportunity for transport and communication industries and these industries tend to attract population. Mechanisation has meant less farm labourers were necessary.

6. Occupation is the nature of the work an individual performs in person.

7. Elasticity is the change in the amount demanded in response to the change in the price of goods.

## Page 29

8. The aim of specialisation is to decrease costs, increase efficiency and enable a price cut in the hope there will be a big rise in demand for a good.

9. The main factor was the introduction of electricity across the country. (So it was available to factories wherever they were located.)

## Page 30

### A. Complete

1. stock

2. one person

3. Any order: banking, finance, transport, skilled labour force, subsidiary firms, research organisations, trade missions

### B. Answer these questions:

1. Ownership of shares needs to be sepa-rated from the everyday running of the company and this is done by having a board of directors. Other problems are the difficulties of managing a large firm.

2. —Horizontal combinations, that is firms who were once in competition amal-gamating.
—Vertical integration, that is bringing various stages of production under one control.
—Lateral integration, that is marketing a product in a different way, e.g., through advertising.
—Overseas markets. Australia sends products overseas to many markets.
—Firms within Australia combining with various overseas firms, e.g., Toyota.

## Page 32
### Answer the questions:

1. Production is an activity directed to the

# Basic Economics Answers

satisfaction of peoples wants through exchange.

## Page 33

2. The productive process is the name given to the way the economy is organised so that the producers are able to supply the goods and services that their community wants.

3. How much producers produce is dependent on people's needs and how much money they have to spend.

4. A wage is a fixed regular payment earned for work or services, typically paid on a daily or weekly basis. The amount may vary according to time worked. A salary is a fixed amount of money that is paid to a person regardless of the amount of hours they work. These are generally paid to people like managers, bureaucrats and politicians.

5. Parent to mark.

6. Parent to mark.

7. It depends on their income and their expectation of what they will earn in the future.

8. They will get into debt.

9. No it is not sustainable. We need to start paying back our debt, spend less and expect the Government subsidies whether in pensions, childcare, family payments etc. to go down.

10. It is neither sustainable or fair.

## Page 37

1. Answers may vary slightly but should include:
   a. Feudal System: land owned by lord
   -serf allotted portion to work
   -in exchange serf worked for Lord for set number of days and paid a percentage of their produce
   -villages self-supporting
   --after Black Death labour was scarce so serfs were allowed to pay in money rather than in labour
   --this led to Lord's changing use of land from wool to wheat
   b. Guild System: merchant guild con-

trolled trade in the interest of the town
   - self-governing
   -controlled quality and prices and bound members to guild rules
   -they decided conditions surrounding transactions and made treaties with other towns
   -apprenticeships were usually 7 years and they received little pay
   -appearance of craft guilds who controlled own craft
   -guilds also responsible for charitable work among members
   —solved disputes
   c. Domestic System: division between capital and labour
   -people paid for what they produced
   -advance in specialisation
   -special types of products were made in different areas
   - start of factory system by assembling workers under one roof.
   d. Factory System: handcraft products were replaced by machine production
   -workers were employed as permanent wage earners
   -employees did not own the equipment or work at any other job
   -power was used to turn machines and factories were located near sources of power.
   -conditions of work and living were very good
   —there was an enormous increase in output and as a result living standards improved and trade spread throughout the world.

2. The Factory System best describes the type of system used in modern Australia.

## Page 40

### A. Match definition

1. d
2. e
3. a
4. c
5. f
6. b

### B. Answer the questions:

1 a. any 3—professional services,

# Basic Economics Answers

education, public administration, domestic services, transport, merchants and retailers, builders and construction

## Page 41

b. any 3: wheat, cattle, dairy products, other agricultural products, fisheries, forestry, minerals.

c. any 3: fruit, vegetables, rice, manufacturing

2. Answers will vary. Parents to mark.

## Page 44
### Answer these questions:

1. Trade unions were insignificant because a large amount of the work was done by convicts who were not paid. Farms were mainly small.

## Page 45

2. Gold was discovered in the 1850's bringing a huge rise in the population. Not every person found gold, and many spent what they had found. People had to be fed so there was an increase in retail. Later, as alluvial gold petered out, workers returned to farms, others took up land and industry slowly started to develop.

3. Trade unions started to develop in the 1850's as labour was scarce, many people having run away to the goldfields. New migrants brought with them from Europe ideas of the English craft unions.

4. In any order. Unions prospered during this period because of rapid economic development and because they had started to combine on a national basis.

5. 1876-1902

6. The failure of the Shearers Union and Maritime Workers strike laid the foundation for the Australian Labor Party. Members of unions felt that the only way they would be represented fairly would be by forming a political party of their own.

7. This Act was important because it was the first comprehensive regulation of working conditions in factories, shops and other industrial establishments. It restricted the working hours of women and children.

8. The maximum ordinary hours for the week are 38 hours and the spread of hours is between 7am and 7pm. (Google: Fair Work Ombudsman.)

## Page 48-49

Parent to mark. Make sure the student has researched and is not just copying facts learnt in this book. References should be included.

## Page 52
### Answer these questions:

1. The Conciliation and Arbitration Act was set up to arbitrate industrial disputes, make awards, interpret and enforce awards and hear civil or criminal cases relating to industrial law.

2. In 1926 the award was changed so that all cases involving the basic or living wage could be heard by a full bench of the Court. A Conciliation Commissioner was also appointed as a mediator.

3. It was abolished in 1956 as the High Court Held that the Conciliations Court could not exercise an arbitration and judiciary role. The Commonwealth Conciliation and Arbitration Commission was appointed to carry out mediation functions. The Commonwealth Industrial Court, which later became part of the Federal Industrial Court, was created to carry out judicial powers.

4. The High Court is the highest court and the final court of appeal in Australia.

5. 2010    Fair Work Australia

6. Changes were made to wage adjustments because it was thought that these adjustments aided inflation since as soon as the public were given more money prices rose.

7. A Margin is the amount paid above the minimum wage for skills and/or responsibilities.

8. CPI stands for Consumer Price Index. It is a measure of changes, over time, in retail prices of a constant basket of

© Valerie Marett
Coroneos Publications

Australian Homeschooling #564
Basic Economics

goods and services representative of consumption expenditure by resident households in Australian metropolitan areas.

9. Answers will vary. Parent to mark.

**Page 54**
**Answer these questions:**

1. Australian banking system is known as branch banking because it has only a few banks but many branches all over Australia.

**Page 55**

2. The Reserve Bank maintains the stability of the currency of Australia; is responsible for the maintenance of full employment in Australia; it maintains the economic prosperity and welfare of the people of Australia through creation of economic stimulus by setting the cash rate, which is the rate at which financial institutions can lend to the public but setting the interest rate.

3. Answers may vary slightly.
Banks are commercial businesses. They offer chequing accounts, savings accounts, and other long-term saving or investment type accounts. They also grant various loans, such as mortgages, and personal loans. In addition, banks have shareholders, and their goal is to make money for their shareholders. Their funds are guaranteed by the Government up to $300,000.

Credit unions and building societies differ from banks as they are owned by their members. They are mostly focused on a particular community, such as a town or suburb, workplace or industry, but are linked together by the ATM network. They offer services such as savings accounts, chequing accounts, loans, etc. Their banking service is not guaranteed by the Government.

**Page 57**
**Answer these questions:**

1. The first bank opened in Australia was the bank of New South Wales. It is still open although it changed its name to Westpac.

2. The development of the wool industry led to the establishment of more banks.

3. Answers will vary but should contain much of the following:
The expansion of the wool industry and the gold rush encouraged the establishment of new banks. Travelling between towns was far more difficult than today so people preferred to have banks nearer where they lived. However, many banks failed due to changes such as the establishment of too many banks, the end of the gold rush and the asset price collapse in 1888. As there was no central banking mechanism the money in the town bank was not secured so the prosperity of the town affected the stability of the bank. During the gold rush gold was transported to banks in Melbourne and Sydney by coach and these coaches were subject to robbery by bushrangers.

4. Answers will vary but should include:
bank notes were not legal tender so were often not recognised outside the town and certainly not outside the state since they were secured by each bank. This meant money or gold needed to be carried when travelling. It also made less easy transactions between businesses.

5. Answers will vary. Parents to mark.

**Page 59**
**Answer these questions:**

1. The Commonwealth Bank was established to carry on the general business of banking in competition with the existing trading banks. As the bank was Federal rather than State owned transferring money between States was easier. The Bank was not established earlier as Federation only occurred in 1901.

2. The Reserve Bank was to carry on the central banking functions previously undertaken by the Commonwealth Bank and to issue bank notes.

# Basic Economics Answers

3. Answers will vary. Parent to mark.

## Page 61
### Answer these questions:

1. The Australian Securities & Investments Commission (ASIC) is an independent Australian government body that acts as Australia's corporate regulator. ASIC's role is to enforce and regulate company and financial services laws to protect Australian consumers, investors and creditors. It is one of three government bodies that regulate financial services.

2. a. **hedge fund:** an offshore investment fund, typically formed as a private limited partnership, that engages in speculation using credit or borrowed capital.

   b. **underwriting** is the process by which investment bankers raise investment capital from investors on behalf of corporations and governments that are issuing either equity or equity or debt securities, ensuring any losses are not born by one company.

   c. **equity:** the value of shares issued by the company.

   d. **brokerage firm:** a financial institution that facilitates the buying and selling of financial securities between a buyer and a seller. Brokerage firms serve a clientele of investors who trade public stocks and other securities, usually through the firm's agent stockbrokers.

   e. **debentures:** a long-term security yielding a fixed rate of interest, issued by a company and secured against assets.

## Page 62
### Define:

1. **statutory fund:** a fund established in the records of a life insurer and relates solely to the life insurance business of the life insurer or a particular part of that business. The money in this fund can not be used for any other purposes than for which it was set up.

2. **fiduciary:** a person or a business, e.g.,

a bank or stock brokerage, who has the power and obligation to act for another under circumstances which require total trust, good faith and honesty.

3. **annuities:** a specified income payable at stated intervals for a fixed period, often for the recipient's life, in consideration of a stipulated premium paid either in prior installment payments or in a single payment.

4. Answers will vary. Parent to check.

## Page 64
### Answer the questions:

1. medical expenses; job loss and unemployment; credit card debt; divorce; unexpected disaster

2. credit card debt and unemployment answers will vary as to why the student thinks this. Parent to mark.

3. Answers will vary. Parent to mark.

## Page 66
### Answer the questions:

1. Answers may vary slightly. Shares are a means of investing in, and becoming part owner in a company in order that your money will increase through the company's growth or/and through dividends paid to you by the company.

2. The main Australian share market is the Australian Securities Exchange.

3. The stock market is the place where shares of publicly held companies are issued and traded.

4. a. **capital growth:** this is the difference in the price shares are bought and the value when they are sold.

   b. **dividends:** the share of the distributable profits of the company in which the person holds shares.

   c. **Capital Gains Tax:** tax payable on the profit, (either the dividend or growth in the share at sale).

Australian Homeschooling #564
Basic Economics

# Basic Economics Answers

5.   You take the risk that the share will lose value.

6.   Answers will vary. parent to mark.

**Page 68**
**Answer these questions;**

1. Superannuation is framework where money paid into a fund is invested towards payment of a pension at a later date.

2. In any order:
   a. **Employer/corporate/staff funds** - these are funds established by an employer for the benefit of their staff.
   b. **Personal funds** - fund joined as an individual through a super provider.
   c. **Industry funds** - these were originally set up for people working in a particular industry, e.g. builders or health care workers, but now often available to anyone.
   d. **Self-managed super funds** (also called 'do it yourself' funds) - these can have up to four members and are generally used by people with larger amounts in super or by family groups. They are managed personally by the group.

3. The present minimum age is between 55 and 60.

4. Governments have made superannuation compulsory so people will be able to support or at least partially support themselves in old age and not be reliant on tax payer welfare.

5.   Answers will vary. Parent to mark.

**Page 70**
**Something to Do**

Parent to mark.

**Page 73**
**Answer these questions:**

1. a. **exports:** sending goods or services to another country for sale
   b. **imports:** bring goods and services into a country for sale
   c. **balance of trade:** the value, over a stated period, of payments received for merchandise as compared with the value of payments made for merchandise imported
   OR
   the value, over a stated period, of current payments made internationally for both goods and services
   d. **favourable balance of trade:** payments received from other nations exceeded the payment made to other nations for goods imported

2. Any of the following: insurance, banking charges etc.; payments for port charges; Australian tourists visiting overseas; Government expenditure, e.g., defence, overseas aid; interest payments to overseas governments and private individuals.

3. Funds are commonly invested in Australia by establishing branches in Australia, purchasing stock or shares or purchasing properties or businesses.

**Page 76**
**Answer these questions:**

1. The International Monetary Fund works to foster global monetary co-operation, secure financial stability, fascilitate international trade, promote high employment and sustainable economic growth, and reduce poverty around the world.

2.   When productivity increases the same amount of labour is needed although the amount of output has increased. Products then become less expensive and the numbers of markets increase, so generally no jobs are lost, and in some cases the number of jobs may increase.

3. To make sure that borrowing from overseas does not lower our standard of living we need to make sure that the money is invested in industries that would make enough profit and export enough products to repay the loan and interest.

4. The advantages are: the lender can import more goods using the interest to cover the cost of additional goods or he can fund further overseas investments.

# Basic Economics Answers

5. The advantage for the borrower is that it allows the borrower to maintain or increase his production and find further markets for his goods.

6. It benefits a country because employment is higher when production increases and the people's standard of living increases.

7. The purpose of the International Bank for Reconstruction and Development is to help developing countries, reduce poverty, promote economic growth and build prosperity.

**Page 77**

8. It fulfills its purpose by providing a combination of financial resources, knowledge, technical services and strategic advice to developing countries.

9. a. **exchange rate:** the value of one currency for the purpose of conversion to another, e.g., Australian dollars to U.S. dollars
   b. **terms of trade:** this represents the value of exports of a country relative to the value of the imports.
   c. **balance of payments:** this is a systematic record in monetary terms of all transactions, which take place over a year, between residents of Australia and all other nations including goods, services and income and transfers such as gifts.

10. Parent to check.

**Page 78**
**Explain these terms give an example:**
(answers my vary on given examples)

a. **tariffs:** duties or taxes levied on goods coming into the country. animals

b. **free trade policy:** an international treaty that allows better Australian access to important markets and an improved competitive position for Australian exports. Japan

c. **embargo:** an official ban on trade or other commercial activity with a particular country. Liberia, Iran

d. **excise duty:** an indirect tax charged on the sale of a particular good.

alcohol, tobacco, fuel

**Page 79**

e. **preference trade agreement:** a trading bloc that gives preferential access to certain products from the participating countries. European Union

f. **protective tariff:** a duty imposed on imports to raise their price, making them less attractive to consumers and thus protecting domestic markets from foreign competition. cameras, computers

g. **exchange control:** a government restriction on currencies between countries. Mugabe, Zimbabwe, Democratic Republic of Korea.

h. **revenue tariff:** a tax applied to imported and exported goods in order to increase the revenue of state or federal government. luxury imported cars, alcohol, petrol.

i. **protection:** covers all types of action by government to give home producers an advantage over overseas competitors. meat, wheat

j. **import quotas:** a physical limit on the quantity of goods that can be produced abroad and that can be imported into a country in a given period. dairy

k. **economic nationalism:** a body of policies that emphasize control of the economy, labour and capital formation, even if this requires the imposition of tariff and other restrictions on the movement of labour, goods and capital. restrictions on animals entering Australia.

**Page 81**
**Answer the questions:**

1. Prior to Federation each state decided its own trade policy. This happened because each state had begun at different times and faced different conditions, settlements weren't large and travel between states was slow. At the time it was probably the most practical way of working. States were fiercely independent and N.S.W. for example would have not understood the

# Basic Economics Answers

problems faced by W.A. As the country developed a single policy was needed.

2. The first tariff board was established in 1921. It had to decide if other forms of protection were desirable; the necessity for new duties and whether duties should be reduced or increased; proposals for new tariff agreements with other countries; questions of costs and efficiency as compared with countries overseas and the effects of additional protection.

3. During the Depression there was a large increase in tariff prices as there was a large deficit in Australia's balance of trade due to the decrease in export prices. Later some imports were prohibited altogether in an effort to stimulate industry and increase employment.

4. Lowest tariff: British preferential tariffs
   Intermediate tariff: for those countries with whom Australia had trade treaties.
   General tariff: merchandise from other countries.

## Page 84
### Answer the questions:

1. —Japan and Australia first traded 1856
   -—Trade interrupted by World War II started again in 1950's
   —2nd largest export market 1956 1957 reciprocal agreement Australian exports and Japanese imports would receive the same treatment as foreign buyers
   —1960's Japan's trade with Australia grew
   —1970's Japan consolidated its position as Australia's major trading partner
   —1980's Australia started to open international trade system and this benefitted Japan
   —1990's substantial purchase of real estate in Australia by Japanese stirred some anti-Japanese feeling
   —1990's Japan leading export partner
   —since 1990's, with Japan's economic slump its dominance of the Australian market slipped

—1994 in coal, beef, gold, iron ore and natural gas Japan accounted for 1/2 of Australia's exports
—15th January 2015 Japanese-Australia Economic Partnership agreement

2. Parent to mark.

## Page 85

Answers will vary. Parent to mark.

## Page 87
### Answer these questions:

1. Government aims to maintain full employment; to maintain a stable rate of growth in the economy; to have a fair and reasonable distribution of income between members of the community.

2. Revenue to finance the governments aims comes from loans and taxes, both direct and indirect.

3. The aims of nineteenth century government was to keep government expenditure as low as possible, thereby limiting government responsibilities; balance the budget and therefore not upset the balance of the economy; taxes should be designed to affect human behaviour and the workings of the economy as little as possible.

4. A balanced budget is one where expenditure and income are equal, that is one balances out the other.

## Page 88

5. The government changed its opinion because it saw the need for social services; economic conditions changed; developments in the field of economic theory; and the GDP came to be used as the primary indicator of the health of a country's economy.

6. Government no longer saw low government expenditure as a good thing; the Budget was constructed according to the current economic situation; taxes were designed to help the economy in various ways.

7. Answers will vary. Parent to mark. Suggestions: No it's not really the

# Basic Economics Answers

government's responsibility to redistribute income. It does not really work as those with more money will find ways around tax laws. While a society should help those in need, many times the poor remain poor because of their spending habits.

8. No we can not afford this. The obvious solution is for Australians to go back to becoming more self-reliant.

9. Answers will vary. Parent to mark.

## Page 92
### Answer these questions:

1. a. **classical economics:** this theory says markets function best with minimal government interference.

## Page 93

b. **Keynesian economics:** in the short run, and especially during recessions, economic output is strongly influenced by total spending in the economy.

c. **demand-side policy:** if people are working the economy is good. If people are not working the economy is bad.

d. **conservatism:** advocates low taxes, reduced government spending, minimal debt, free trade, deregulation of the economy, lower taxes and privatisation.

e. **libertarianism:** maximising individual rights and minimising the role of the state.

f. **Austrian economics:** the belief that economic performance is optimised when there is limited government interference.

2. The GFC was a global financial crisis. It affected all the advanced nations.

3. Any order:
   — National Building and Jobs Plan
   — cut in official cash rate
   — well regulated and supervised financial system
   — Government guarantee for deposits
   — Reserve Bank based monetary policies
   —sharp fall in the Australian dollar

—10.4 billion fiscal stimulation package
—15.2 billion COAG package
—payments to low and middle income earners
—investment in schools, housing, energy efficiency, infrastructure, roads and support for small businesses

4. Answers will vary. Parent to mark.

## Page 95
### Answer the questions:

1. a. **taxable income:** is tax on a person's assessable income less any allowable deductions

b. **capital gains tax**: tax imposed on any gains from assets under a specified period

c. **superannuation tax:** a minimum level of superannuation an employer must pay to their workers' retirement fund

d. **fringe benefit tax:** tax imposed on the non-cash benefits provided by employers to employees

## Page 96

e. **Medicare Levy and Surcharge:** payment to Australia's public health insurance scheme

f. **goods and service tax:** broad-based tax of 10% on most goods and services sold or consumed in Australia

g. **tobacco tax:** all tobacco sold is taxed

h. **fuel tax:** fuel tax applies to all fuels in Australia including petrol, diesel, oil and lubricants

g. **tariffs:** taxes applied to goods imported into Australia

h. **luxury cars:** flat 33% tax rate when a luxury car is sold or imported into Australia

i. **agricultural levy:** the levy is collected to provide money for research, development and marketing of agricultural products

Australian Homeschooling #564
Basic Economics

# Basic Economics Answers

j. **alcohol tax:** rates of tax vary with different types of alcohol for the purpose of recovering the cost of alcohol related harm and education on the harmful effects

2. Answers will vary. Parents to mark.

3. Answers will vary. Parents to mark.

**Page 99**
**Answer these questions:**

1 a. **debt ceiling:** this is how much the Australian Government can borrow and set by Federal Parliament

  b. **net debt:** the sum of all liabilities, less their assets

**Page 100**

  c. **deficit:** spending more money than is received in revenue

  d. **fiscal balance:** the difference between revenues and expenditure

  e. **surplus:** the amount of money left over when all Government expenditure has been met

  f. **interest:** money paid regularly for the use of money left

  g. **national debt:** accrued federal government deficits over several years

© Valerie Marett
Coroneos Publications

Australian Homeschooling #564
Basic Economics